# ANXIETY ACROSS THE AMERICAS

One Man's 20,000 Mile Motorcycle Journey

by Bill Dwyer

Second Edition, November, 2014
First Printing, April, 2013

ISBN-13: 978-0615760216
ISBN-10: 061576021X

Cover Art by Katie Stinman
Editing by Elizabeth Green (elizabethgreenwriter.com) and Sean
Michael

# TABLE OF CONTENTS

# ACKNOWLEDGEMENTS

Each of you made an impact in making my dreams a reality.

Amber, Mom, Dad, Elizabeth Johnston, Matt Johnston, Lois Pryce, Ted Simon, Roseann Hanson, Jonathan Hanson, the Overland Expo, Ara and Spirit, Mandy Jane, The Cartel Coffee Shop, Elixr Coffee, The Pope House Bourbon Lounge, Bell Helmets, Aerostich, my online audiences, HorizonsUnlimited.com and Google Maps.

Thank you for all your support in each of your unique ways.

# DEDICATION

To Amber,

for watching me leave,
and taking me back.

# PROLOGUE

They say you never see a motorcycle parked in front of a psychiatrist's office. The expression refers to how motorcycling can be good for the mind, soul or whatever you call it. Five years ago I started riding motorcycles, and two years ago I started seeing a shrink. I was pessimistic, cerebral, and overall, a miserable guy. That's who I was, and continued to be until my "quirks" grew to an unhealthy level. I slipped into a deep depression with bouts of mania, and that's when I sought help. I was diagnosed with manic depression along with a generalized anxiety disorder.

My depression was episodic and medication helped, but my anxiety was a constant presence, a fundamental part of my personality. A key characteristic of my anxiety disorder was an excessive and uncontrollable worry over everyday matters. After I started getting better, I realized how bad things had gotten. There wasn't an easy fix and the doctors stressed that I can't be cured, it's just the way I am, but I can learn how to cope with it. I had been riding motorcycles for years and without knowing it, been coping with my anxiety through this hobby. I never bought my first motorcycle with the intention of traveling, but soon day trips turned into weekend trips, then week long, and now I'm chucking it all to live on the road. It was exposure therapy for all the things I feared, like social situations, spontaneity, making decisions, and the unknown in general. Life on two wheels challenged me in these areas and if I hadn't discovered motorcycles I'm sure I would have been laying on a shrink's couch years earlier.

I pull into the parking lot of my shrink's office. That old saying pops into my mind and I smirk. I have some news for him. I'm early and the cheerful receptionist greets me in the same way she has for the last two years.

"Hello, William! He'll just be a minute. Would you like to

schedule your next appointment in the meantime?"

"No thanks, I'll just wait."

"Okee dokee!"

This is my last visit and suddenly I'm reminded of my initial evaluation two years ago. He started with general questions about my background and was constantly scribbling notes.

"Are your parents divorced?"

"No."

"How would you describe your relationship with your parents?"

"Good. I mean, we're not incredibly close, but we have a good relationship."

"Do you see them often?"

"Couple times a year. I fly back to Chicago where they live."

"How long have you been in Phoenix?"

"About a year."

"And you grew up in Chicago?"

"Yea."

"What is your occupation?"

"I'm a software developer."

"Do you like it?"

"I like the work when it's stimulating, but it's hard to come by usually."

"Where do you see yourself in five years?"

"Five years? Who knows? But in two years I am going to ride my motorcycle to the city of Ushuaia in Argentina. It's the southernmost city in the world."

He scribbles longer than usual then pauses.

"What's in Ushuaia?"

"I don't know. What's in between here and there is what concerns me mostly. It should take about eight months."

He silently chauffeurs me to the office before closing the door and starting our session with the same question he always asks.

"How are you feeling?"

"Good. Great really."

"Good. Why great?"

"Well, I just gave notice at my job that I am quitting, and in a month I am leaving for Argentina by motorcycle."

"Really?"

"Really."

"So you're doing it after all."

"Yep."

"How does your girlfriend feel about this?"

"Well...not great of course, and things are difficult between us right now as you can imagine."

"Sure."

"Originally I thought we would just break things off, and see where we stood until I got back. It seems a little too black and white though. So we are going to keep in touch so that I'm not showing up eight months later like a stranger."

"Well, good luck with that."

"Thanks, we'll see."

"So are you ready?"

"Yep, got the bike, gear, savings, and vaccinations."

"How's your Spanish?"

"Non-existent. I'll study and pick it up along the way."

"I'm sure you will."

This is the first of many future goodbyes.

---

Jenny was sold to me from the son of an Alaskan who happens to live in Phoenix. She is a 2001 Kawasaki KLR650, a single cylinder "thumper" as some say. She is a little top heavy with her six-gallon gas tank sitting high, but overall she is comfortable and easy to fit with luggage. Most of the modifications I planned on doing are already done. She is ugly and banged up, which is exactly what I was looking for. Even if I could afford it, I don't want to be riding around on a shiny, expensive motorcycle. I imagine I will be perceived as a big dollar sign on two wheels as I ride through lesser-developed areas. This is one of many things I imagine before my departure.

The KLR model hadn't been changed in 20 years, which says to me that the design is solid. She isn't amazing at anything in particular, but she is good at everything. Off-road, highway or around town, she can handle just about anything. They call Jenny's model the "Swiss Army Bike" of motorcycles.

I want to get accustomed to her before the big day. During many trips throughout the US, I get to know her. We come to an agreement about things. She overheats above 100 degrees when I push her revs high. She tells me what her range is like by cutting the engine on the highway. I swerve back and forth to slosh the gas from the left side of the tank to the right, where the input hose is located. She doesn't have much to say, usually, but I always listen when Jenny speaks.

I never removed the Alaskan plates, or got her registered. I have been parking my other motorcycle (Marla) illegally in Phoenix for the past three years without getting ticketed. Maybe I was just lucky. I won't be so lucky when I am faced with dozens of border crossings. I need proper registration so officials can confirm I am the owner. I never got the title transferred and three months before my departure I start jumping through all the legal hoops. This is the first used vehicle I bought and I didn't realize I needed the signature of the owner to transfer the title. I try and track him down. I call his cell phone and the line is dead. I call his girlfriend whose number I got from an email: another disconnected message. I email him half a dozen times. No reply.

I can't find the title either. I lost it. I go to the DMV and see if they can contact the previous owner. It's three months to go and I've screwed up everything already.

The son who sold it to me must have moved. Since Jenny is registered in Alaska I contact their DMV and commissioned research to have a clerk track down the last known address of the owner. If his father is still in Alaska, I have a chance at getting a new title and transferring it.

Three long weeks pass and I get the address of Jenny's previous owner. I mail a letter to the Alaskan and another three weeks pass without an answer. I have six weeks before I need to leave. I already informed my employer of my last day at work and I have no legal ownership of Jenny. I am frantic.

I start looking up what I could get for Jenny if I strip her down and sell her parts individually. I haven't stolen her, but I am ready to turn my parking space into a chop shop. Maybe I can get enough money from selling her parts to buy another KLR. My girlfriend Amber tells me to wait, and says everything will work out. I reluctantly listen to her.

The vehicle identification number is marked on the engine and frame. For the next week I look for KLR owners with cheap bikes for sale. If I transfer ownership of another KLR to my name, even if it's not running, I can replace everything with Jenny's good parts. I spend hours preparing for this backup plan.

A week later I receive a call from an unknown number. It's the Alaskan. Amber wonders what the hell is going on as I jump up and down in the living room like a mute kid at Christmas. He apologizes for the delay of his response. He was on vacation for the previous month. I thank him profusely and apologize for letting this situation happen in the first place. I put away my hacksaw and socket set. No need to cannibalize Jenny.

# DAY 1
# PHOENIX, ARIZONA, USA

"Do you know there's a road that goes down Mexico and all the way to Panama?--and maybe all the way to the bottom of South America... the road must eventually lead to the whole world. Ain't nowhere else it can go--right?"

On the Road by Jack Kerouac

Latitude:   033° 26' 54" N
Longitude: 112° 04' 26" W

20,000 miles to Ushuaia

---

The start of my journey begins at a gas station for that final top off of fuel to keep me going far on the first leg. Stopping for gas 45 minutes after you've started takes away the forward momentum. I go out of my way to my favorite gas station. It has fast credit card authorization, clean pumps, functional keypads, quick fuel flow rates and always a fresh set of towels and washer fluid to clean off my bug ridden helmet visor. It's these little things that matter when you're riding around in 110-degree heat with a one-piece motorcycle suit.

I'm good at creating routines and systems to make things run more efficient. On an average day, a stop at the pump is like changing tires in a racecar pit, and I can fill up in about two minutes if I don't snag my glove on something. But this isn't my average day, so I take my time. I watch others going about their day and their own routines. The moment I gear up and fire up the engine marks the start of one of the stupidest or greatest things I will do in my life. The situation is banal and momentous at the same time. There is no audience, no going away party, just me and Jenny and we pull out of the station as anonymously as we entered. And just like that, my adventure begins.

I left Amber, my girlfriend of one year, a few hours ago. I shuffled around the apartment soaking in the last remaining minutes I would have with her while she got ready for work. Our goodbye was short and bitter. It was just like any other day except I would not be home when she returned. I tortured myself by imagining her walking in the doorway and the sadness that would overwhelm her. I would return after this whole thing, if she would have me. I love her dearly and leaving her is the hardest part of this journey's beginning.

Panic quickly set in after the sound of Amber's car engine faded in the distance. I left my girl, friends, job and everything I know to travel by motorcycle to Ushuaia. I was on the verge of shaking and one thought echoed in my mind:

"Jesus Christ, what the hell have I done?"

Ushuaia is considered to be the southernmost city in the world. It resides in the Argentinean state of Tierra del Fuego, which largely makes up the southern tip of South America. It is only 5,000 miles away from Antarctica and the winter temperatures of the southern hemisphere rival Alaska's. I am planning on arriving in the trailing summer month of February or March where temperatures are hospitable.

I don't know much about the city itself and there is nothing that draws me to it. I am more concerned with what is in the middle. The foreign countries, people and languages are what intrigue me, the unknown. That's what's what I want to point my front tire at. A weeklong trip into Mexico or even a month throughout Central America doesn't seem to be enough for me. I want to immerse myself in Latin America for a long period of time and eight months seems enough. My savings won't allow for much more anyways.

In Phoenix I was a software developer and had been for six years since I graduated college. I showed up for work, did my job and went home. In every job I hold, I show up later and later for work in the morning as the months go by. It's not because I'm not a "morning person" (which I'm not), but after a certain period of time, things turn routine, boring and lack a challenge. These circumstances make me unconsciously and even consciously oversleep until the last possible moment. "Forty-five minutes late isn't grounds for termination" or "I haven't even received my first write-up yet," I would think to myself half asleep as I hit the snooze again. Fortunately my line of work allows me to come late and stay late in most circumstances, and an understanding boss is helpful too.

The intrigue of the unknown is half of my motivation for this journey. The other half is the sheer challenge of it all. I have avoided the "American Dream" like a plague and the exorbitant debt that accompanies it, so my bills are minimal and easily paid on time. I can afford simple luxuries and besides my job, I have little responsibilities except for my two cats, Guff and Belle. Life for me is easy, too easy.

I want to throw myself out into the world and see how I will fair. I begin to see this as a rite of passage; a test of whether I am capable of handling whatever situations life throws me into. I don't know Spanish and I only know the basics of motorcycle repair. It only seems natural to ride 20,000 miles through Latin America. I have my challenge.

I am no stranger to motorcycles though. About four years ago I learned to ride in my hometown of Chicago. A friend of mine taught me how to ride in a parking lot near my house. I started on my Mom's 2001 250cc Yamaha Virago and my Dad's 1987 750cc Virago. My friend owned a 2002 750cc Suzuki Katana with more power than my parent's cruisers and after a couple of weeks of practice in the parking lot I timidly asked if I could take his for a spin. "Sure," he replied as if it was no big deal. The bike's power intimidated me and I ran it around in the parking lot to get a feel for it. I finally took it down the block to stretch the bike's legs and see what she could do. On a long straightaway I cracked the throttle open with some more vigor and she took off. The experience was so visceral. The noise from the wind roared over my ears, the wind left my body tingling and my eyes focused on the road and its contours with a level of concentration I had never experienced before. My senses were absolutely consumed. I glimpsed down at the speedometer and it read only 30 MPH. This was the moment I decided to buy my own motorcycle.

In the summer of 2006 I bought a brand new Kawasaki Ninja 650r. It is a mid range bike with an emphasis on touring. A "sport tourer", they call it. I chose this bike because it felt comfortable. I had not intended on traveling long distances when I bought it. For my first year I had only ridden around the surrounding areas of Chicago and sometimes the inner city. I liked curvy roads but they were hard to come by in the gridded streets. In downtown Chicago the 25 MPH "S curve" on Lake Shore Drive was my favorite. I would take the half hour ride from my suburban home around midnight when traffic was light so that I could take the curve at a spirited speed.

It wasn't long before I was traveling beyond Chicago. Day trips turned into weekend trips. Eventually I was taking week long journeys through the Appalachians and a two week cross country trip from Chicago to Phoenix where I moved in August of 2008. The southwest offered much more scenic opportunities than the prairies of the Midwest. I began reading a lot of motorcycle adventure literature by popular authors like Lois Pryce and Ted Simon. They inspired me deeply and the length and frequency of my travels increased. My thirst for exploration seemed unquenchable. Holidays like Thanksgiving were no longer spent with friends or family. I remember sitting on a curb in the middle of nowhere eating a turkey sandwich from a gas station feeling truly at home. Along California's Pacific Coastal Highway 1, watching the sun set over the ocean near Big Sur with the Bixby Bridge in the foreground was my piece of heaven. The last day of a trip was always the worst when I headed back home to the "real world".

I don't know exactly when the last day of my journey will end. There are very few time-sensitive plans. There isn't much of a concrete plan at all. I learned throughout my years of traveling that the best trips are those with the least amount of structure. With no expectations there are no disappointments. Serendipity is the best road map. I have a general idea of what order I will pass through each of the countries in Latin America, but besides that I will figure it out as I go. The first leg will take me to my hometown of Chicago. It's a 3,000 mile detour and I'm tempted to enter Mexico through Baja, but seeing family and friends before I leave is more important. I don't have any test rides with Jenny fully loaded so if any problems occur they will be easy to mend in the states.

---

"This is it, here we go," I say to no one as I leave the gas station. I head east on Interstate 202, the expressway I used so frequently over the past three years. To the left is my old apartment and to the right is Tempe Town Lake, an artificial construct in the middle of the desert. The lake is empty because the dam broke a week earlier and I wonder if it will be full again when I get back. Memories flank me and remind of the good life I'm leaving. Doubt and regret fills my mind, but the wheels are already in motion, literally. I preoccupy myself with the list of last minute things I needed to do before I cross into Mexico. New tires and a chain will carry me to Panama. I still need to find a spare heavy duty tube to carry in case I get a flat that can't be patched. I am rolling down the road, but I haven't let go of all the planning and preparation. It's as if I am sitting at my desk at home, but with 60 MPH winds. I pass by a trail Amber and I hiked to see the desert's springtime bloom. It was one of the best days we spent together and witnessing the sign for the turnoff rips me open. I'm crying and blubbering like a baby in my helmet. Unable to wipe the tears due to bulky motorcycle gloves I let them evaporate in the wind and absorb into the cheek pads of my helmet. I wash the salty remnants from my face in the sink of a gas station bathroom and stare at the man in the mirror.

"What the fuck am I doing?", I ask him.

I glance down at the odometer every 30 seconds. It feeds my insecurities. It says to me, "you are 100 miles from the comforts of home. Now 110. Now 150."

I stop and put a piece of duct tape over it. The odometer is the figurative "check engine" light of my fragile psyche. I ride long into the night as if I am trying to escape the force of my former home's gravitational pull. I am looking for an event horizon where there is no turning back, implying that if I leave the state, then I might as well carry on all the way to Argentina. I chose the Arizona/New Mexico state border. "Just make it over the border, Bill," I keep saying to myself. It's a 19,000 mile rationalization I convince myself of in order not to turn back. I cross the border and set up camp at an RV park. The sympathetic owner gives me a reduced rate. I think he senses I am having a rough day. Being a fairly stoic man, the emotional roller coaster I had ridden today left me exhausted. Anxiety has been building for months and today I reached a tipping point where emotions broke free. I sleep like a baby.

The anxieties of the previous day melt away and I eagerly pack up to hit the road. I take back roads north into Colorado at a more relaxed pace. Around sunset I spot a sign for a mineral spa resort that reads "Campers Welcomed!" I turn down the road to check it out and pull up to park next to a path leading to the office. I cut my engine to restore the peaceful ambiance around me. The tall gate I push open doesn't lead to the office. It's the back entrance to a mineral spa. Dozens of people are bathing and others walk around in matching pink and blue bathrobes. With helmet in hand, in my dirty red one-piece motorcycle suit, I clomp over the deck of the pool to the front office. Looking like someone from a post apocalyptic era, I try to diffuse the confused look on the man behind the counter with a bright smile.

"So it says you have camping spots here?" I ask.

"Yes sir."

"How much for a motorcyclist? I just need room for a one person tent and my bike."

"Twenty five dollars, sir."

"Yikes. I'm just looking for a safe place to sleep for the night. I don't need any of your amenities. Any chance for $15?"

"Sir, our camping spots are at a fixed rate."

"I just need a piece of earth and $25 seems a bit steep for that."

"Sir our camping spots are--"

"OK, OK I got it, thanks anyways."

Jenny's single cylinder thumps away as we pass the Zen garden and ride out in search of another spot to camp. A few miles down the road we find a trail through an open field. Tucked behind some shallow hills I set up camp a mile from the road. I am fortunate to witness two beautiful spectacles happening at the same moment: an orange sun sets in the west while a big yellow moon rises over the hills in the east. If I wasn't a cheap ass I would be staring at the side of a log cabin instead of this wonderful sight.

I stop in Denver to stay with a friend for the night. She and her housemates are preparing to go to Burning Man, a huge festival in the middle of the Nevada desert. They invite me to come with, and I consider it. It is 1,000 miles in the opposite direction of what is already a 3,000 mile detour. Some other time.

I blaze a trail across Kansas to St. Louis where another friend is putting me up for the night. I plan on riding throughout the evening with a full moon keeping me company on the deserted road. The sun sets and the dusk fades. I stand up on my foot-pegs to stretch my legs and notice my headlight is out. So much for riding throughout the night. In 20 minutes I will be riding blind. I ditch my plans for a late night ride. Maybe this is a sign to call it quits after a long 400 mile day. I pull off onto a dirt road to look for places to camp. I see some tall grass and a couple of trees between two fields. It will have to do. After setting up camp I diagnose my faulty headlight down to a simple blown fuse. I scold myself for not checking it right away on the side of the road. I could have made it to St. Louis tonight. Lesson learned. Curling up in my bivy sack sounds pretty good at the moment anyways. Safe in the obscurity of the brush I fall asleep to sounds leaking from a raucous tavern in the distance.

After a short stay in St. Louis I head north. The first sign I see for Chicago gives me goose bumps. I am happy to see family and friends, but I begin seeing this stop as the final one before Mexico, which I am anxiously waiting to enter.

After a week and a half in Chicago I get too comfortable. Amber urges me to hit the road, insisting I'll never get this stupid thing over with if I keep "dicking around" with my friends. I say my goodbyes to everyone and most of them feel like they are giving me a last goodbye. "I'll be fine," I insist, especially to my Mom.

Violence along the Mexico border from drug trafficking is surging and commonplace in the news. Stories of civilian decapitations and images of vehicles riddled with bullet holes is what comes to mind to most Americans when they think of Mexico. Here I am heading straight for it. Their worry is no surprise. "Be safe," most would say as if I am going into a war zone.

With futility, I attempt to switch the perspective on some.

"Oh, I'll be fine. It's you I worry about. Chicago's crime rate is the fastest rising in the nation. I just hope to make it out of here alive!"

I'm the only one who finds this funny. The security situation in Mexico is exaggerated, but it is still a reality. Everything I'm bringing with me is disposable, including my motorcycle.

"What if someone takes your motorcycle?" a lot of people ask. "Then they will have my motorcycle and I go home." I say.

I try not to preoccupy myself with too many 'what if' questions.

On the way to St. Louis I stop at my sister's who I haven't seen in awhile. We catch up and I am reminded what it's like to be an uncle for a few days. My niece looks up to me, and I get this weird feeling that I'm an adult. We're not so different. I just have bills.

On the day I leave, two miles from her doorstep the rear tire starts to feel squishy and my handlebars begin to wobble. I pull in my clutch and slowly come to a stop on the side of the road. I have a flat rear tire. Great way to start the day. I take this as an opportunity to test my roadside tire changing skills. The valve stem is ripped off so the tube can't be patched. I rest Jenny on her side as I begin to wrestle the rear wheel free. It's a Sunday morning in the countryside and naturally there are a lot of bikers out for a ride. It takes me 90 minutes before I fix up Jenny, but 30 of those minutes are spent with people stopping to see if they can help. Jenny is tipped over, so most thought I crashed. A caravan of bikers with rubber necks, whipping towards the spectacle that is me, almost cause an actual crash when one rider brakes and another doesn't notice. He locks up his rear wheel and screeches down the road. I finish the repair and start heading south. No more detours.

In St. Louis shipments are waiting for me. Once again, two miles from a doorstep I have another mechanical problem. After I exit the expressway I make a sharp turn and the chain rolls off the rear sprocket. "Aw c'mon!" I shout. I am so close to the end of a ten hour day on the road. I unkink the chain and seat it back on the rear sprocket while rolling the bike forward. "C'mon Jenny, just a couple more miles..." I plead with her. The chain rolls off every couple blocks on side streets and the last two miles take me an hour.

At the house I rip into the packages like a kid at Christmas. Four millimeter tubes, knobby tires, new chain and sprockets! Oh boy! I install all the new parts over the next couple of days. Knowing that these are the last familiar faces I will see for a long time, I feel hesitant to leave.

There is one more package I forgot to open. It contains two Spanish Bibles. I got the idea from somewhere to pack them in case I get kidnapped. I can claim I am a religious missionary and pity would be taken on me. It seemed like a good idea at the time. I attended 12 years of Catholic school and yet know nothing about Catholicism. What if they grill me about the Stations of the Cross, or ask me to recite a Hail Mary? Now that the books are in my hands I realize my foolish paranoia and leave them behind. When my rationalizations to stay run out, I leave my friends and head south for the border.

I am a couple days away from the border. I decide to try "couch surfing." The website, CouchSurfing.com allows people to search for places to stay while traveling, as well as open up their own home to weary travelers. The online community is self policing like eBay. Hosts with couches to be surfed on, along with surfers, establish reputations from feedback they receive. I have no experience so I want to try and build up my reputation in the US.

The first couch I surf is in Dallas, Texas. I plot a course in my GPS and zig zag my way towards strangers who are kind enough to open their home to me. The neighborhood looks safe, but I am still far from the house. Street after street the houses grow larger and more elaborate. Eventually, my GPS leads me to a mansion. "This is too good to be true," I think. I sheepishly knock on the towering door and I'm greeted by the people I corresponded with online. "We like to surprise people," they say with a grin. They have more than just a couch for me. With only three people living there they give me the "east wing". An entire wing with a billiard table, pool and home theater to take advantage of. It's been a long day and I just want a place to crash. They are great company and incredibly hospitable. The extravagance of the quarters is a rare case, but an amazing first impression to the world of couch surfing.

After another positive couch surfing experience in Austin, I stay in Eagle Pass on the Mexico border. I am filled with a mixture of anticipation and anxiety. I have to talk aloud to reassure myself.

"This is what you wanted Bill, an adventure. Quiet the voices of those who've never been and listen to those that have. Everything is going to be ok."

Only a week ago I was reassuring my family and friends, and now I am doing the same to myself.

# DAY 31
# PIEDRAS NEGRA, MEXICO

"The cave you fear to enter holds the treasure you seek."

Joseph Campbell

Latitude:   028° 41' 52" N
Longitude: 100° 31' 28" W

15,503 miles to Ushuaia

My "comfort zones" don't typically manifest physically. It's something I use to define a bunch of things that weird me out. Talking to women, dancing and NASCAR are close to the top of my list. If you find me dancing with an attractive woman at a NASCAR tailgate party, I am probably sedated, drunk or both. I have the luxury of seeing the boundary of my comfort zone in front of me. First virtually on the screen of my GPS as I ride toward it, and soon before my eyes. I am crossing the Mexico border.

Piedras Negra is the border town in the state of Coahuila. The stark change of the atmosphere is dizzying. Within one mile I travel into the wild west, but with a Latin flair. Traffic laws disintegrate and the largest vehicle has the right of way, contrary to what the signals read. As a motorcyclist, the odds are not in my favor, but the agility of Jenny affords me other advantages. I split down between the rows of cars to keep the wind flowing through my suit in the desert heat. Soon I am free of the town's hustle and bustle, and the road opens up.

I don't have to stop until I reach the immigration office 30 miles from the border. I specifically chose this crossing because of this. A surge in violence along the border had begun a couple months ago, and spending the least amount of time near it feels like the best move. I haven't spoken to anyone yet. I walk into the empty immigration office without knowing any Spanish. I get my visa and import Jenny with relative ease, but the reality of the language barrier hits me with full force as I fumble through conversations that often break down to pointing and nodding.

It is nine o'clock in the morning and I am 300 miles from Monterrey where I will be couch surfing with Carmina. She speaks English and I hope this will allow for a softer landing in the country. I am on schedule and feeling good. The desert landscape is hardly different from parts of Arizona. The familiarity of it is comforting in a land where everything is new.

I pass through a town where the speed limit slows to 25 MPH, but everyone is easily doing 60. I stay with the flow of traffic so I don't get bulldozed by trucks. At the edge of town the traffic thins out and I relax in the right lane. Ten minutes later I see a police car behind me and its lights are flashing. How long has he been there? When was the last time I checked my mirrors? Maybe he's pissed after tailing me for so long. I can't hear sirens over the wind and music playing through my headphones. It's my second hour in Mexico and I am already getting pulled over. I see no populated areas up ahead so I pull over in a remote spot off the road.

A smiling officer greets me with a handshake and asks for my license. My ear is barely tuned to the Spanish language and even a word like "licencia", very similar in English, falls deaf on my ignorant ears. He forms a rectangle with his fingers and then mimics how one turns the wheel of a car. It's quickly apparent that I don't speak Spanish and he calls for another officer in the car. He seems to have more seniority and speaks into a walkie-talkie as he approaches. I notice the silver six shooter hanging off his belt and then a third officer walks into my blind spot. Despite the anxiety welling up inside me, I manage to wonder if silver six shooters are a standard issued piece for officers, and how cool that would be if it was. I snap back to the reality of the situation. The walkie-talkie looks strange to me. I am baking in the heat with my leather gloves and jacket and all three of them are on me before I can even get off of Jenny.

I take my helmet off and place it on my mirror. It is equipped with a lipstick sized camera attached to its side. The recording device is mounted to Jenny's handlebars. I keep the camera rolling and face it towards the officers and me.

With English that is about as good as my Spanish the senior officer tells me that I was speeding. The rest of Mexico is speeding as well, but they pick me. I can't articulate how I could not obey the speed limit in that traffic without putting myself in danger. For ten minutes the officer tries to tell me something, but I don't understand. Visibly frustrated, he goes to his truck and returns with a notebook. I adjust my helmet to frame the shot a little better. The type of camera I am using is set to a mode intended for continuous recording, but if I don't press the "tag" button every five minutes the footage will not be saved. I compulsively press the button every two or three minutes and the officers are not bothered by this or just don't notice it.

The other two officers are circling the bike and inspecting my luggage cases, perhaps imagining what might be in them. The senior officer starts drawing in the notebook. First a stick figure and he makes it clear that this represents me. Above the figure he writes "500". What is happening is starting to sink in for me. I ask, "Pesos?" (about $50 dollars). The officer shakes his head no and adds "dollars" to the end of the "500". God damn it.

I use the first Spanish verb I learned to make my first lie to a foreign police officer. "No tengo!" (I don't have) The officer returned to the figure and started to draw bars over it. My heart sinks, and I can feel him watching it shrivel. I still protest and say, "No tengo!" I write "100" in the notebook and say, "tengo", trying to haggle. The officer shakes his head back and forth, walks away and swings his arm in a "come along" motion. I think I am going to jail.

I cave and ask him to give me a minute. I walk to the opposite side of Jenny where I have exactly $500 stashed for emergency purposes. I adjust my helmet to frame up the shot and hit the "tag" button before I dig out the money. My heart is pounding and I'm on the verge of shaking. I don't want to go to a Mexican jail. What happens to Jenny if I do? Whatever I can do to not go to a Mexican jail, I do it. I find the money and hand it to the officer. He scolds me, "Pay a-ten-si-on! Pay a-ten-si-on!" and I apologize profusely. He waves me off like he would a dog and they leave in their truck.

I'm sweating, shaking and tingling with adrenaline, but my mind is preoccupied with one question: "did I get it on tape?"

I am giddy with laughter as I review the footage to find that the whole situation was captured. Even the money exchange too, a literal "money shot." Suddenly the officers return. I am confused and scared even more than the first time. What's the problem now? The dull-looking heavy-set officer that stayed in my blind spot gets out and yells something at me. I notice an empty plastic bottle he left on my luggage. Maybe he has come to retrieve it? I span the distance they keep from me and hand him the bottle. He throws it to the ground and yells at me some more, waving me away. I realize that they want me gone and to stay gone. They sit and stare as I pack, suit up and ride off.

My pockets are $500 lighter but my spirits are soaring. Capturing police extortion on video is the most interesting piece of footage I shot since I started documenting my journeys four years ago. I have to wait until I exit Mexico before I can put it online. If the video goes viral I may be a wanted man by other police officers throughout Mexico. I push on to Monterrey.

---

Carmina, my Couch Surfing host, makes up for my first impression of Mexico. I arrive in Monterrey, and park my bike in front of her apartment. I try to make myself look less like a hobo and comb my hair in my mirrors. Ten hours of riding gives me some pretty nasty helmet hair.

"Ahlo Beeeil!", Carmina shouts from four stories above.

I meet her on the stairs and extend my hand. She scowls at this gesture and greets me with a big hug, like I'm family. I meet her sister Christina and their two cats, Solovino and Saskatia.

I spend the first two days in the apartment and only venture a couple blocks to a shopping center to run some errands. The culture shock is kicking in, along with the reality of this journey I just started. The break-neck pace of Monterrey's streets and my complete lack of Spanish skills don't help either. Wherever I go I feel like I am being watched by people. I feel like an outsider, a target, a fool.

I spend a lot of time on my computer, uploading videos and photos. I am receding into my comfort zone. During this fragile state, Carmina is great at easing me into Mexico and reducing my anxiety. She cooks traditional meals and explains the why's and how's of everything. We go out into the city, and later that evening we go to a party too. She's an amazing host. We take a trip to a historical town outside the city with her boyfriend, Esteban.

Carmina narrates the story behind every building, meal and sight. I plan on staying for just the weekend but I extend it for a week since they insist. I hope the kindness of these strangers, now friends, is not a rare occurrence.

It is difficult to leave the apartment. Carmina has the type of kindness that can restore your faith in humanity, even after being shaken down by the police days earlier. Outside those doors lay the chaos of the streets of Monterrey, and I'm intimidated. I point Jenny south and stay on the major highways. The conditions are better than I expected. The road is like glass. Jenny and I hum along at 60 MPH. This is a comfortable speed for a single cylinder engine with luggage that acts like sails in the wind. Other cars speed by us at twice the speed and I'm constantly checking my mirrors. I feel like I am on the German autobahn, just swap the Ferrari's for Ford F350s. A military truck with a dozen soldiers is crawling up a steep hill. I cut my speed so I don't whiz by it because I think this will invoke suspicion. As I overtake the truck the soldiers focus their attention on me. Their faces are fierce but battered and tired from the heat. I don't like guns and I get weirded out when they are near. The soldiers have machine guns hanging from their shoulders. The attention I receive is short lived and they dismiss my presence quickly. "Another gringo on a bike", I think they think. Despite the guns, I feel safer in their company.

I pull off the highway onto a cobblestone road that leads to a depleted silver mine. This is the first rough patch of track I encounter since I started, and my inexperience is showing. My hands are aching, a sign that I am gripping the bars too tightly.

The leading cause of motorcycle accidents is the nut that connects the saddle to the handlebars. Human instinct is contrary to the proper operation of a motorcycle. It took a lot of exposure before I overcame those instincts. For example: 1) lighten your grip when the front tire seems to be wobbling out of control, 2) accelerate when you feel a loss of traction, and my favorite, 3) to turn left, turn the bars to the right (a phenomenon called counter-steering). The path of a motorcycle can often continue safely on its own without the input from a rider. It's a rider's survival instincts that threaten their survival.

My instincts are kicking in and I am gripping the bars too tightly. I bring my anxiety out into the light of consciousness and loosen my grip. "I'll let you do the work. You know what you're doing," I say to Jenny.

I reach the town of Real de Catorce. It's the home of an abandoned silver mine. It costs $2 to pass through the 1.5 mile long mining tunnel. The width of the tunnel allows for only one direction of traffic to flow at a time, but for motorcycles this is not a problem.

Jenny and I can squeeze through almost anything. The air in the tunnel is crisp and cool. Jenny's cylinder thumps and echoes in this otherworldly atmosphere. I exit into a market onto a pedestrian path, unsure if motorized vehicles are allowed. A smaller bike passes and weaves through the people, so I follow suit. On the other side of town I ride Jenny through the remnants of a bull fighting circle. Jenny has the power of about 34 horses and I wonder what the bull to horse conversion rate is. Two to one? Maybe three to two. In any case, I am pretty sure Jenny's presence marks the record for most bulls fitting in this ring. I see a good place to camp near a clearing behind a cemetery. I kill the engine and the silence is deafening. I decide to spend a few days here.

My neighbors in my campsite are six feet under, so I sleep well. In the morning, I poke my head out of the tent and notice two police officers nearby. They are just standing around chatting, but their presence makes me nervous. I lay in my tent hoping to wait them out, but nature calls and I emerge from my tent. I can feel their eyes on me, and I give them a wave that they return. It's my first time camping in Mexico, and I start cooking breakfast as if everything is normal.

"You're alone, cooking breakfast in a cemetery in the Mexico countryside, and everything is going to be ok," I say to myself.

The last part of that statement is key: "everything is going to be ok". No matter how much I am freaking out inside, if I stop and tell myself that, or even say it aloud, it drops my heart rate.

They come by to say hello, and watch me cook for a few minutes before they are on their way. Everything was ok, just like I said it would be.

As I walk through the market, men offer me donkey rides into the hills with the promise of peyote along the way. I'm on a big enough trip already and decline their offer. I soak in the peace this mountain town has to offer before I head south.

I arrive in San Luis Potosi at Jose's house. I am couch surfing again. His mother answers and is unaware of the arrangement. I know her son's name and that's enough to welcome me into her home. Jose is on a camping trip and was supposed to be home yesterday. The mother shrugs in a way to suggest, "Jose will be Jose." His brother is there and shows me around. Their house is beautiful and they insist I bring my motorcycle indoors. I don't want to dirty up the floors and the four steps I have to ride Jenny up makes me nervous. The mother insists, and I don't argue with her. I fail on my first attempt. I am too hesitant and slow. I give Jenny more gas and rocket up the steps. My momentum carries me well past the threshold. I slam on my rear brake and skid to a stop in their living room where two small doxen appear from nowhere barking at me.

I rest for the next few days and enjoy the comforts of the indoors. I haven't spent a nickel on lodging since I entered Mexico. Camping is fun but wears on me after a while. I wake up nauseous one morning and can barely get out of bed. Jose's Mom brings me tea and it helps. Jose's brother invites me to a party he is going to that evening. His salsa class is getting together to celebrate the end of the semester and I take him up on his offer.

As we drive to the party I realize a fact that strikes terror in me. I am going to a party full of salsa dancers. There's a good chance there will be dancing, of the salsa variety, and I'm a terrible dancer. We walk in, six packs in hand and I dart my eyes around the kitchen for a bottle opener to get the social lubricant flowing. Everyone speaks English, but I try and keep up with the Spanish they speak among each other. Friends, pizza and beer; things don't change too much across cultures. I enjoy watching everyone interact, so full of life. There are a dozen people and it's not long before the radio brings everyone to their feet over a favorite song. The guys are pushing the furniture against the walls and everyone starts partnering up. I hope their vision is based on movement, and if I stay very still they won't see me. I accidentally make eye contact with a girl across the room.

She's pulling at my arms trying to get me to dance.

"But I'm very bad," I say.

"But I'm a very good teacher," she snips back at me.

"I'm a lousy student, too."

She simply smiles at me and I rise to my feet like the sucker that I am. She takes me through the motions. 1-2-3...4-5-6 and repeat. My neck is at a right angle, looking at my feet as if it's my first time seeing them. When I am not out of sync I am stepping on her toes. I try to retreat to my seat, but she doesn't let me. I step methodically, 1...2...3......4...5...6. I take a few more steps and even more swigs of beer. I start to feel the pattern and suddenly I'm doing it. I'm salsa dancing!

The night before I leave Jose's, he returns from his camping trip. I'm acquainted with his whole family more than the guy who invited me in the first place. I am unable to stay up late since I have to leave early in the morning if I am going to make it to Guanajuato where I'll be couch surfing again.

The map of Guanajuato is a spaghetti bowl of roads and my GPS is useless. I am trying to find Sanje, my host for the next few days. Attempts to call him from a pay phone fail. I try every combination of country, area and mobile codes I know and I keep getting the same, erroneous recording. I find an internet cafe and finally get directions from him through email. I hail a cab, hand him a piece of paper with the address, and ask if I can follow him.

I can barely keep up with the cabbie, but ten minutes later I'm there. I'm looking for apartment D32 and the numbers and letters change order with each building. I can't see any pattern. Little children are playing soccer in alleys and I ask them if they know where D32 is. A little boy points me in a direction. I ask the next group of kids and then point me back in the direction I came.

I've reduced the search area down to a couple square blocks. I opt for the brute force method and start traversing every alley, and all of its branches. A half hour has passed and I round one of the last corners. My shoulders whip back and I hear a deep growl. A dog lunges and bites my backpack. I struggle to get him off, but he only loosens his grip until his master comes and tells him to stop. I stumbled into a private area of residence. I apologize to the owner and call off the search for Sanje.

My sunlight is fading and the only hotel I saw was for $60 a night. I ride twenty miles outside of the city to stealth camp. I find a pullout on the side of the road with a small trail into the woods. I ride Jenny along it until she can't be seen from the road. The ground is sloped so I sleep in my hammock. The next day I head back into town to search for a place to stay. I'm leaning on my motorcycle on the street, while I formulate a plan and a man notices me. We start chatting and I ask him if he knows any cheap places to stay. He happens to run a hotel and 20 minutes later I'm relaxing in my room located in the heart of Guanajuato.

I spend a few days exploring the city and adjusting to the culture shock. I practice ordering food, and study my Spanish dictionary. In the central square I notice a fellow solo traveler with pasty white skin to match. She's got hiking boots, a backpack with a dozen pockets, and clothes that probably haven't been washed in a few days. She pulls out a travel guide book and it's a sure thing that she's not from around here. I spend ten minutes working up the nerve to talk to her. It's been a week since I've had a conversation that wasn't in broken Spanish. I move to the bench she's sitting at and say, "So you come here often?" My stupid line is enough to break the ice and we get to talking. It feels good not to strain myself to express a thought as simple as, "nice day". We agree to meet for breakfast the following morning. Her name is Hana.

Things between Amber and I are not going well. We're not completely together, but we're not broken up. I have no phone, so when I find internet access my first message is to her. She is incredibly supportive, but also very hurt from my departure. I am emotionally checked out, and I compare her troubles to mine.

"I'm sorry you are lonely, but at least you know where you're sleeping every night and when your next meal is," I say with scorn.

My empathy for her is fading against the escalating obstacles I face each week, and I am growing more cold towards her. An email conversation has spiraled outside the bounds of decency and it's ended with a single response that needs no reply.

"I can't do this anymore," Amber's email reads.

I meet Hana for breakfast the next day. I'm sad, and she can tell, so she asks what's wrong. I recount the events that lead to the last email and suddenly I'm confiding everything to this stranger I met just yesterday. We exchange information to keep in touch. She's on her own adventure through Latin America by bus, and I wonder if our paths might cross again. I head south towards Mexico City and clear my head in the wind atop Jenny.

# DAY 47
# MEXICO CITY, MEXICO

"You just had a near-life experience!"

Fight Club by Chuck Palahniuk

Latitude:   019° 25' 57" N
Longitude: 099° 07' 59" W

14,141 miles to Ushuaia

---

Mornings are full of packing and I am getting really good at it. I do it with a military-like precision, and from the time I wake up it takes a half hour until I'm on the road. It's a long day of riding. I want to avoid Mexico City. At 20 million people it is tied with Seoul, South Korea for the second most populated metropolitan area. It has about a million more people than New York City, but less than twice the area. The pace of Monterrey was too much for me, so I just want to get past the city. Three hours north, an old BMW flies by me and waves. Motorcyclists often wave to each other when passing. It's been the first one  since entering Mexico. He has New York plates and a dog on the back seat. I reach a tollbooth just north of the city and I see the BMW on the shoulder. I pull up next to him and exchange greetings. He asks where I'm headed and I tell him south of the city. He laughs and says in this traffic it could take me four hours. I had already been riding for 10 and I cringe at the news. "You can stay at my place if you like", he says. It takes me only a few seconds to consider and I say, "Sure, thanks!" I realize we hadn't even exchanged names. I shout, "I'm Bill, by the way!" as he pulls away and he shouts back, "Oh, right, Nick!"

I follow Nick into the traffic. I can tell right away he knows how to ride. His bike is faster than Jenny and I have a hard time keeping up. We split down traffic lanes backed up for miles. There is a clearing in traffic and Nick accelerates to an unknown speed. His speedometer broke months ago. I am scared of losing him and Jenny is chugging away with a wide open throttle. I change from the left lane to the center. Nick is already in the far right. During the lane change I ride over a small berm in the road formed by heavy trucks. My handlebars start to wobble. I take my eye off Nick and see 80 MPH on the odometer. My bars are still wobbling back and forth. Only my fingertips are in contact with them. "Come on Jenny, straighten out." The wobble is not going away. I accelerate and the wobble turns into a tank slapper. The bars are violently shaking to the left and right. The front wheel deflects too much for the bike to stay upright. Jenny and I go down on our right sides. We separate from each other quickly as we slide down the road. My hands search for something to hold onto, something to bring this terrifying slide to an end. The sound of my helmet scraping along the cement drowns out the metal shrieking coming from Jenny up ahead. Nick hears it and sees the cloud of dust in his rear view mirror. I continue sliding down the road. My weight is distributed onto my hip, butt, hands, and boots. The road is straight and smooth. I come to rest 100 yards from when I fell. I stand up in the middle lane of the three lane expressway. I glance ahead first and see Jenny careening off to the side of the road. Then I check behind me to see if any vehicles are bearing down on me. Cars in each lane miraculously slow down evenly. They saw everything and reacted perfectly. I sprint to the shoulder and drop to my knees. People pull over and rush to my aid. They ask me if I am ok, but I don't know.

Everything happened so quickly. I had no time to process it. The expressions of people in the crowd are a mixture of concern and confusion. They had just witnessed me sliding down the road at 80 MPH. They are staring at a ghost. How am I standing?

I am ripping off my clothes, searching for signs of trauma. Nothing. I grab at my limbs, and punch at myself hoping to invoke some sign of pain over the adrenaline surging through me. One of my cases was destroyed and half of my belongings are scattered across the road. Bystanders help me gather my things.

I run up to Jenny and get her upright. Besides a bunch of scratches and a broken highway peg there is no major visible damage. I hit the starter and she sounds strong but isn't turning over. A minute later she roars to life and I start laughing. "Fucking bullet-proof these KLRs are!" I spend a half hour resting before I am following Nick through the concrete jungle again. I am jacked with adrenaline still. Nick's engine is overheating and we stop a couple times to let it cool. It takes almost two hours to get to his place on the south end of the city. He shows me my room and mentions that he and his housemates are having a party tonight.

At the party I am introduced over and over as the "guy who almost died four hours ago." I tell my story a dozen times throughout the night and watch the same cycle of surprise, shock and concern wash over the listener's face.

I am replaying the event over and over, not reliving it. My body had a near death experience, but my mind shut down and all I remember are the events before and after the crash. I had a near death situation, not experience, and I feel cheated. My life didn't flash before my eyes and I haven't come to any poignant realizations about life.

I'm sitting on a couch with a beer watching the party run its course. The banality of life is amplified against the backdrop of death and maybe that's my realization. My philosophizing falls by the wayside as women grow in numbers. I start wondering how my unique story can get me laid, and suddenly life isn't so banal. Like most of my attempts at sexual conquest, I get nervous, drink too much and pass out.

I am woken up by a sharp pain in my right hip. Adrenaline and the booze staved off the pain and my bruises start to show their color. I decide to take it easy and spend a couple days resting. Nick and his roommates have no problem and I spend the next ten days in Mexico City.

I spend a day trying to track down a new luggage case. My right one was destroyed in the crash. It is a well known brand around the world and the model is fairly cheap at $120 in the US. I visit a string of camera shops in downtown Mexico City, but they are all dead ends. As I pass the massive center square I notice a bus full of police drive by, then a second, and a third. I notice the riot gear as I hear an explosion in the distance. Everyone else resumes their business and I wonder if I am the only one noticing the beginning of a riot. I find out that an organized protest is up ahead and they happen on a daily basis. Locals don't flinch at the sound of smoke bombs. Streets are being blocked off by police and I can't exit the square the way I entered so I take a moment to rest in a cathedral. A thin metal wire hangs alongside the towering columns and ends with a plumb, hanging over a seismograph. I realize this is used to detect the slightest movement the seemingly immovable pillars make over time. I love churches, particularly in Latin America. They offer me a sanctuary from the constant noise. I sit and reflect on the things I've gone through in so little time. Police extortion, salsa dancing and near death. Six more months to go. Maybe the worst is behind me now. The explosion of a smoke bomb echoes through the church breaking the peace and I exit into the busy streets.

---

Next stop, Oaxaca. I stop to camp in the mountains off a lonely stretch of road. The solitude is refreshing and I bask in the silence. I have a small stove and can cook my meals as long as they can fit in a two cup pot. It can burn the same fuel Jenny uses too. More importantly though, I can squeeze an extra ten miles out of Jenny should she run out of gas in the middle of nowhere with my one liter fuel canister.

I arrive in Oaxaca where I intend to spend a few days helping out a local school with their computers. I wander around the city for a place to stay and see an expensive BMW sport bike parked on the sidewalk. Half the time I think of Jenny's safety before mine. If a $20,000 Beemer is safe here, I'm sure she will be too. Before I cut my engine the owner is peeking his head out the window. Jenny's sound sets her apart from most bikes in Mexico. The man needs only a glance at me and Jenny to know we are far from home. Chris, the BMW owner, introduces himself and it turns out he's from Canada and runs the hostel. Two motorcyclists far away from home: instant friendship.

I spend the first day at the school fixing printers, updating drivers and networking computers. It's easy work and I enjoy watching the children run around. The next day is filled with more of the same, but I have alternative motives. I want to try and make a lasting impression. An open source software project provides students with all kinds of learning activities and I hope it can aid in their education. I don't often see opportunities in life where I feel my actions can make a measurable improvement in people's lives, but I dream of putting tools in place to create a richer educational experience. I see a chance here and want to try to do some good for a change.

It's training day. I speak to a group of teachers through a translator. I explain the system and give a demonstration of the exercises. Their faces are blank. I am not making a good case for the value of the system. I start to give examples of how it can be used in a lesson plan and a few start nodding their heads. I bring up the reporting tools to track a student's progress and the noises of approval start coming from the staff. I wasn't impressing anyone when I was explaining the exercises, but when I started talking from their point of view I was speaking their language, albeit through a translator. I feel like I am getting through to them. All I can do is give them the tools and from there it is up to them. I leave with the hope that my work might produce some results.

There are other volunteers at the school and I get to know some. I meet a girl named America and suddenly I'm infatuated with her. I'm flirting with her for all the wrong reasons. I want to mess around with her primarily for the material it would generate for my jokes.

"America plays hard to get."
"America is a sloppy kisser."
"I got to third base with America."

She wasn't interested in me though. America rejected me.

# DAY 66
# SAN CRISTÓBAL, MEXICO

"The nomad does not feel stable when stationary,
he only feels stable when experiencing velocity."

Deleuze and Guattari

Latitude:   016° 44' 11" N
Longitude: 092° 38' 17" W

13,245 miles to Ushuaia

---

I am heading towards San Cristobal for the Day of the Dead. When I pass through towns there are no signs to tell you to slow down. Instead, at either edge a large speed bump is placed. If you are lucky it is painted and visible from a distance. A two lane freeway with trucks speeding above 90 MPH suddenly comes to a 10 MPH crawl for the speed bumps. Jenny and I have negotiated hundreds of these since entering Mexico and I spot them every time by now.

What used to be a teeth rattling surprise has turned into a fun obstacle. I learn a trick to rocket over these bumps at 50 MPH and it's fun as hell. Right before a bump I hit the front brakes hard and Jenny's weight shifts forward to compress the forks. At the peak of the compression I rock on the throttle to shift her weight to the rear tire. I use the momentum from the rebounding forks to lighten the load on the front tire. Sometimes I am able to lift her tire off the ground. All of this is timed so that the front tire can hit the bump and absorb more force than it normally can without bottoming out.

I hit a bump that is bigger than I expect and with my thumb on my GPS the jolt sends the map's cursor way off course. The screen turns blue and the label reads: "Pacific Ocean". "Hey, the ocean!" I say to Jenny. I realize I haven't seen an ocean yet so I divert my course to Salina Cruz.

I find a shipping dock and not much else on the shoreline. The water is freezing and the torrents of waves make sounds that rival the most ominous thunder I've heard. I ride a couple miles from any sign of vehicle tracks for a secluded place to camp. It's my first time with Jenny on sand and she is sinking like a stone. I find a camping spot and keep Jenny upright using my tin drinking cup to prevent the kickstand from sinking. The lights from oil tankers and cargo ships sit statically against the foreground of the violent waves. I sit there for a long time watching them crash over and over. It's like watching a struggle, as if the land has no business coexisting alongside the ocean.

I arrive in San Cristobal two days later and coast down cobblestone streets. The atmosphere is from a simple time, but all the modern conveniences are available. I walk the streets and listen to a movie called *My Dinner with Andre* that is largely made up of dialogue. One morning I stumble across a BMW rally that is meeting a couple of blocks from my hostel. Forty shiny BMWs are lined up along the street like an armada. I park Jenny at the end and take a picture. The caption in my head reads: Which one is not like the other?

The riders are eating at a buffet in the hotel's restaurant across the street. Sure that I will regret the bill I continue for the company. "These are my people" I think to myself. It will be nice to swap road stories. I walk in the dining hall with helmet in hand and the top piece of my riding suit hanging from my waist. My two month old beard is starting to look scraggly and my riding suit is filthy. Between the clinking and chatter one by one each table turns their eyes on me and I feel like my presence is unwanted. I retreat to a secluded area, like the kid no one wants to sit with in the lunchroom. It's high school all over again.

As I eat alone I examine my expectations. Did I expect a party in my honor? A slap on the back? I have just ridden clear across Mexico alone, and yes I do want a party. I want recognition. Keeping to the delusion I have built up in my head I start judging everyone.

"I bet they shipped their bikes down here, or rented them. Their protective gear looks brand new. Where's the battle scars? These guys aren't REAL riders. They've just got a lot of money and pay their way through for a cushy ride. This is the cruise ship version of adventure riding. There's no adventure in it at all!"

I finish eating quickly and grab a second helping that I stick in various pockets of my suit.

I walk along examining the forty bikes to corroborate my previous judgments.

"Look at those chicken strips! Half of these haven't even been dropped. There's not a scuff on them. If you've never dropped your bike you're doing it wrong."

I spot a couple exceptions from the bunch. They are dirty, scrappy, and stuck with stickers from many countries. "These are the REAL riders." I scoff at the "tourist tourers". They are not "hardcore" like me.

Even though my head has grown twice in size over the past 30 minutes I manage to fit it into my helmet. Jenny and I ride away with an air of superiority.

"Come on Jenny, we don't need them. We don't need anyone!"

Tina, a friend I had met at Nick's in Mexico City is in town for the Day of the Dead as well. She is with her friend Alexandra and it's our first time meeting. Her voice remains at the same dull tone that makes her genuine excitement about something sound sarcastic. I think she has a dry sense of humor like myself and delivers her jokes in a deadpan style. After some time I realize her wit isn't dry, it's nonexistent. We are walking around the city when Alexandra spots a guided tour shop. She wants to sign up for one that is leaving tomorrow. I hope this is a sarcastic exception, but it's not. It is an 11 hour trip in a small van through the mountains where eight of the hours are spent cramped into a van. I reluctantly agree. This is why I like traveling alone.

First stop, Agua Azul where the water is a muddy brown instead of a crystal blue as it normally is. I jog ahead to explore the river and come across a steel cable with a cage you sit in to pull yourself across the river. I stash my electronics in the bushes in case I fall in the river and hop in the cage. I release the wheel lock and gravity takes me to the middle of the river where the cable sags. Being a couple feet above the water I realize the river's current is moving really fast. If I fall it will probably swallow me up and bang me against the rows of the waterfall I had been taking pictures of earlier. I eventually cross the river. It takes longer than I think and the van is leaving soon. As I make my way back to the other side a park official screams at me to return. I make it back and he scolds me for putting myself in danger. Still grinning from the cheap thrill I say, "But it's fun!" He is not amused. He tells me that I have to pay a fine. My Spanish suddenly vanishes. I apologize, say I have to catch my ride and start jogging away.

Second stop, some Mayan ruins with an extraordinary historical significance that I don't care about. It's hour five in the van and my morale is too low to appreciate the site.

Third stop, a giant waterfall the group decides to spend only 30 minutes at. I am spellbound and want to spend all day here. A dead tree lays perched over a lake the waterfall formed. I have to climb this, but the mist makes the trunk incredibly slippery. I reach the end of the tree and there is no clear sign of how deep the water is. I have to jump off this because I am a sucker for cheap thrills. I fall the 30 feet and my landing is free of collisions with any rocks. I check the clock and get as many dives in as I can. It is the best part of the whole day and now I am holding up the van with my antics. I climb back into the cage that has four hours of mountainous roads to traverse back home. It was all worth it for those 30 minutes.

The next day is the Day of the Dead but there are no festivities as we expect. We go to a cemetery where family members decorate the graves of their loved ones they've lost. It's like a party to most. They put food on tombstones for the dead. A little girl opens a soda bottle and places it on a grave as family members laugh and play. It was his favorite soda. Something that I found so morbid as an outsider now appears sweet and loving. The familial bonds are stronger than I have ever seen.

I am not close with my family. We are not on bad terms. We simply don't share things like feelings and intimate thoughts. It's more so the case that I don't share. I am incredibly introverted. I am materially wealthy compared to most in Mexico, but they are rich in relationships and I find myself jealous.

I am entering Guatemala tomorrow and I'm just as nervous as I was before crossing into Mexico almost a month ago. Another unknown territory to plunge into. I am getting too comfortable and for me it's a sign to move along.

# DAY 72
# QUETZALTENANGO, GUATEMALA

Andre:   Our minds are just focused on these goals and plans,
which in themselves are not reality.
Wally:   Goals and plans are not... they're fantasy.
They're part of a dream-life.

*My Dinner With Andre*

Latitude:   014° 50' 10" N
Longitude: 091° 31' 19" W

13,007 miles to Ushuaia

---

I am heading towards the city of Quetzaltenango where I am taking two weeks of Spanish lessons. Five days for five hours a day with a private tutor: $170 a week. This includes three meals a day cooked by the family I am staying with. Not a bad deal.

My command of the Spanish language is largely based on road signs. I can talk for hours if the conversations are narrowed to the rules of the road: school zones, speed limits, speed bumps, dangerous curves and U-turns. Good to know while riding, especially the speed bumps, but not useful for most conversations.

I arrive at the school and the headmaster greets me. He speaks in slow and soft Spanish and I get the gist. The papers are signed and my admittance is official.

"Bienvenidos!" he says.

"What?"

I can see his face sink. He's simply trying to say "Welcome!" It's the most common sign I've read on the road for the last month but my ear has never heard it spoken. I have a lot of work to do.

On Monday morning I arrive to school with Jenny and everyone notices my entrance from her loud exhaust. Miguel is my assigned teacher and he calls me a robot based on the way I look in my motorcycle gear. We're in a small room, 6 feet by 4 feet for the next five hours, and it's a little weird.

I tell him my story, where I'm from and where I am going. He flips to the end of my notebook and starts sketching a motorcycle. Arrows are being drawn to the various parts with their Spanish translation.

| | | |
|---|---|---|
| wheel | clutch | headlight |
| tire | air filter | exhaust |
| motor | battery | seat |
| brakes | spoke | tank |

I have an index for Jenny's parts so I can explain any problems. It's a great way to bridge the language barrier and the most fitting first lesson I can imagine.

The family I am living with for the next two weeks is incredibly hospitable. There are two other Spanish students from Denmark living here as well. Breakfast, lunch and dinner are served at 7:30 A.M., 12:30 P.M. and 5:30 P.M. on the dot. Family and students gather at the long wooden table and a flurry of Spanish makes my head spin for the first few days. My lessons are helpful and soon I am actively listening. Into the second week I am starting to participate, but I mostly ask about what certain words mean. Knowing how to ask what you don't know is the first step towards knowing.

I find a cafe to work at while I'm not studying for school. Workers are mopping around my feet and I realize it's closing time. I've been here for six hours, editing clips from the footage I shot of the Mexican police officers threatening me with jail. It's been almost a month since it happened and I've been waiting to upload it until I exited Mexico.

I try and keep the video objective. I don't want this to be another negative story about corruption. I don't want this to be a representation of all of Mexico. It's simply something bad that happened to me and the potential for it happening to others is real. So I leave a cliffhanger at the end and tell people that the next video I publish will discuss how to handle these situations, but I am still figuring out the answer myself. When I met Nick in Mexico City, I told him what happened with the cops and how they got $500 from me.

"I would have gone to jail!" he said.

I felt like a sucker and that I caved into their demands way too easily to let that much money go. In the video I lie about the amount and say they demanded $100 dollars so I don't appear to be a complete pushover. My sense of pride is stronger than I realized. I publish the video online and wait to see what happens.

Throughout the week people set up shop in the school to sell their blankets. I'm uninterested at first until I notice a blanket the right size for Jenny's saddle. I find a pattern Jenny would like and buy it. In the evening I spend a couple hours wrapping the blanket around her saddle and securing it with bailing wire. Now she has some Latin flair to her.

On the weekend I join a group from school to hike up Santa Maria, a volcano overshadowing the city. We will be camping overnight at the summit, 11,000 feet up, so I pack a lot of gear. I treat this as a trial run for my hiking setup before I enter Peru and attempt the four day hike on the Inca trail. There is a six month waiting list to hike the trail and I don't have a reservation, but I assume I can arrange something when I get there. Believing something will happen is the first step towards making it a reality.

It takes six hours to make it to the summit. I have wobbly legs and a dizzy head from the altitude. The straps from my backpack have been digging into my shoulders under the weight of my gear, but it's freezing and lugging everything up here was worth it for a warm bed and a hot meal.

Camp is ready before sunset and most of my group members retreat to their tent to escape the wind. Hours later I hear a group of voices in the distance. They sound strong in numbers, and I walk around to investigate. I find the source and a group of people are chanting. There are 40 people in a circle with a man reading from a bible. The flashlight he shines on the pages illuminate his face, like he's telling a scary story. It's too dark for anyone to notice me and I sit with the group just inside the circle. The ceremony continues as women prepare meals in large pots, fueled by coal they carried to the top. I don't know what they are chanting, but the sound of all the voices hypnotizes me. I leave after a break in the ritual and return to my camp.

I am well rested in the morning. The fog has cleared and the sunrise reveals our position above the clouds. My feet are planted firmly on the ground but I have the perspective from the seat of a plane. The others in my group didn't sleep well. Most didn't have warm enough gear for the cold. I fire up my stove and make hot tea for everyone and become a hero for an hour.

Our descent takes two hours and even less for the local children skipping down the trail bare-footed. I feel their stomps before I hear their laughs. I pass an old man slowly making his way up a slope with a bundle of sticks twice his size. The load is on his back and held in place by a band that wraps around his forehead as he hunches forward. I am amazed by these people. Guatemalans are among the most poor in Central America and yet they are all smiles and full of energy. I look forward to exploring the rest of this country.

I arrive early at school to check my email. I find it flooded with hundreds of comments on the video I posted a week ago. It has been viewed 50,000 times in the last 24 hours. I am giddy with excitement and scramble to find the source of all the traffic. I track down the digital trail to local Mexican newspapers and eventually find that I am on the front page of the El Norte in Monterrey, the Reforma in Mexico City and the Mural in Guadalajara. These are the largest newspapers in all of Latin America.

I can barely focus on my lesson. I share the news with my instructor and we spend an hour talking about it. I return home for dinner with the family, and I share the news with them. I show them newspaper clippings and their eyes widen.

"You are famous!" they shout, laugh and slap me on the back.

I have a lot of work to do and excuse myself to go to the café.

I am fixated on the commentary of my video. The majority of the comments are in Spanish and I can make out some of them. Most are apologetic and ask me not to take this as a representation of Mexico as a whole, which I don't. I try and translate the articles with little success. I make a plea online for interpreters and a half hour later I've got clear translations.

I ditch my last day of classes to make the most of the publicity while I can. Univision, a Spanish television network, emails me for permission to air my footage on their news show, Primer Impacto. I run around to copy shops to get the forms signed and scanned to make things official. I spend most the day refreshing web pages and answering emails. It's not long before I start imagining bounties being put on my head. The bell rings and I have to go to class.

Tomorrow I will leave for Tikal. I glance at the maps, but don't pick any particular route. Things will work themselves out.

I say goodbye to the family, another goodbye among many. I thank them profusely for their hospitality, the mother especially. She sees students coming and going all the time. She is used to it and I've gotten more attached to her than she has to me. She is preoccupied with one of her dozens of responsibilities before I turn to leave. After two weeks of staying in one place my momentum is zero and it is just as hard to gain speed as it is to slow it down.

I stop at the coffee shop that has become my second home here to check up on developments in the news. The state of Coahuila is under the eye of the nation. The mayor says investigations are in the works. People online are saying the radio the officer used is not police issue. Officers sometimes have ties to the cartels and this is one of the ways they communicate.

I've had a personal locator beacon logging my location this whole time. I turn it off and remove the map from my website. The chances of a pissed-off cop tracking me down through the Americas for revenge seemed unlikely, but a cartel is international. Others have been killed who have shown the slightest opposition.

The next article reads, "The three officers have been fired."

This makes me a hero in people's eyes, but I feel like a target now. All roads funnel down to only a few border crossings. If I were a vengeful cartel wanting my blood I'd tell a few people to hang around the borders and look out for me. Maybe they don't give a shit about me. Maybe this is just my ego. Am I assassinate-able?

I had just gotten comfortable, and now I have drug cartels with bounties out for my head. I have no proof of this, but my psychological state is the same with or without. Getting lost in the back roads of Guatemala sounds pretty good right now. I hit the road as quick as I can. Before I hop on Jenny I cut off the sign on her tail that advertises my website, "AtlasRider.com" and toss it in the garbage.

---

Tikal is an archaeological site home to many temples and is thought to be the central urban center of the Mayan civilization. It will take me a few days to make it there from Quetzaltenango. The main routes across the country are mostly dirt and spiral through the mountains. The road narrows down to one lane frequently. Large busses and trucks use these roads, and I wonder how they manage to pass through when opposing traffic meets. I round a corner to meet a truck backing up in my direction to let an oncoming bus pass, and my question is answered.

I've been riding all day and my pace is half of what I expected it to be. I remind myself to get out of the habit of having expectations. There is a sign that I can't read but it seems to be warning traffic to turn off the established path. When in doubt, stay straight. That's my motto in these situations. A mile later I understand the sign. A landslide of massive proportions has swept away the road. The end of the road is a sheer drop where the slide has claimed its way. There are no towns in sight and humans seemed to have dodged nature's bullet on this one.

The slide is a mile across. I make my way back down the road and take the detour, full of technical turns that I've never experienced before. In the middle of the valley, I cut Jenny's engine and bask in the silence. It looks like a bomb went off here. Car sized rocks are strewn all over the land, and the trail weaves around them. I try and imagine what the sound of half a mountain giving way is like.

I am near Tikal but won't make it there before the park closes, so I search for places to camp along the road. I pass by what seems to be abandoned property. I double back to check it out. The concrete walls are still intact but the roofs are gone. There's fresh cattle dung everywhere. There are concrete slabs scattered around and I find the least smelling one out of eyesight for Jenny and me. I wonder if these buildings were meant to have a roof in the first place. The floor of a building with three walls is covered with shit. Maybe it is a staging area. I nestle up in my hammock with anticipation for Tikal tomorrow, and hope the cows don't come home tonight.

I pass a snake-crossing sign ten miles north of the park entrance. A turkey-crossing sign is next, then a deer-crossing. Nothing new to me. The next sign takes me awhile to recognize from a distance. It's a jaguar-crossing. The jungle I have become so comfortable with is slightly more unsettling. Nonetheless I smile at the prospect of an encounter.

I have a few hours before the park closes and I use it to scout the area. I'm wearing shoes that have a thin rubber sole with articulated toes because I like walking barefoot. Just a mesh fabric covers the top of my foot. The ground is soft from the rain and mud squeezes between my toes. The park is huge and I begin jogging to cover more ground. I drown out the sounds of the jungle with some music I chose to be my Tikal soundtrack weeks ago. The Brazilian group is called Uakti and they are performing a work by Philip Glass. They make their own instruments. The drums and wind instruments are the most pronounced. The music amplifies the ambiance, and my steps sync with the beats.

I run past breathtaking temples and take only a few moments to look up at them. I'm too preoccupied with the next four steps I need to make. If I let my attention slip I can easily sprain an ankle on one of the many tree roots or rocks. This is why I love running through forests. It forces you to experience what's in front of your face. No time for wondering what's for dinner, how to get back or what time it is. It is similar to motorcycling in a lot of ways. I run until my lungs burn, and then I run some more.

My head is dizzy and I am at the foot of Temple IV. I am going to return here for tomorrow's sunrise. The sun has set and dusk is gone. Luckily I have a full moon to light my way. I give the music a rest and soak in the sounds of the jungle as I walk towards the exit. Twigs crack around me and I am reminded of the jaguar-crossing sign.

I have this acceptance of everything and so I'm not alarmed like I normally would be. I've wrestled with my 15 pound cat back home and he's gotten the best of me at times. At an average weight of 150 pounds I would have no chance against a jaguar, but I would at least like to make him work for his meal and leave him with some battle scars. With an imaginary fight in mind, I walk out of the park with my knife in hand, flicking it open and closed, and wondering how many seconds I would last.

I get up at 4:30 A.M. to watch the sunrise from Temple IV. It is the tallest temple in the park. Three other temples poke through the canopy in the foreground of the sunset. The park officially opens at 6:00 A.M. and sunrise is at 6:05 A.M. It takes a half hour to reach the temple so I need to get in earlier. I reach the gate entrance and spot the guys on guard. There are five of them and they've been up all night drinking and playing cards as evidenced from the beer bottles covering the table. I walk past them as if it's no big deal, but a guy calls me over. He tells me that the park opens at six o'clock but I ask if it is possible for me to enter earlier. He rests his arm on his shotgun like one would a staff and says that for $12 bucks I can enter. I only have $10 on me and offer him $8. He takes the $8 and brings the shotgun to his knee, pointing to the remaining $2 in my wallet. I tell him it's for food with an expression of pity. He swaps his shotgun for a beer and shoos me away with his hand. I start jogging for the temple and chuckle at how far I've come in negotiating with armed men.

I jog to Temple IV taking pleasure in the fact that I'm the only one in the park, but at the summit there are 15 others who are doing the same thing. They bribed the same guards I bribed. Not a word is spoken and everyone stays silent. We are listening to animal calls echoing throughout the jungle. It is hoarse, low and full of bass. I thought it might be jaguars while I was jogging. Four or five groups were bellowing back and forth at each other, but it turns out to be howler monkeys. They can be heard two miles away and this is how they mark their territory.

The fog is too thick and the sunrise is unimpressive. The howler monkeys stop their calls soon after the canopy lights up and I am left hypnotized, with a moment of clarity. There is no particular subject matter upon which I have a clear perspective, but my senses are jacked up. I hear each sound with blistering lucidity and see each sight with an acute vividness. The others leave and I stay to try and hang onto this feeling as long as I can.

# DAY 95
# PLACENCIA, BELIZE

"The traveler sees what he sees.
The tourist sees what he has come to see."

G.K. Chesterton

Latitude:   016° 30' 49" N
Longitude: 088° 22' 00" W

12,363 miles to Ushuaia

---

I have mixed feelings about visiting Belize. I don't know where to go, it adds 200 miles onto my 600 mile detour to Tikal, and it is an English speaking nation which threatens the progress I've made in my two weeks of Spanish lessons. I go anyways because I want to find a beach to snorkel. When am I going to be around here again?

The immigration officer furrows her brow when I speak Spanish to her.

"Sir, we speak English here," she scowled then studies my passport. "Sir, where are you coming from?"
"Guatemala."
"Sir, of course you are, it is right over there. Where is the origin of your travel?"
"Oh, America through Mexico and then Guatemala by motorcycle."

She studies my passport some more.

"Sir, there is no entrance stamp for Mexico."
"Really?"

"Really, sir."

"They must not have stamped it."

"Well how did you get here, sir?"

I point at my motorcycle, "By motorcycle."

"Sir, you did not enter Mexico. Did you ship your motorcycle at any point?"

I ask to see my passport.

"OK, I see there is no entrance stamp for Mexico, but here is the exit stamp. It's fair to say that I can't exit Mexico without entering it, right?"

She glares at me, then moves on.

"Sir, where are you staying?"

"Belize City."

"Sir, where in Belize City are you staying?"

"Oh, I don't know."

"You don't know, sir?"

"I haven't made any reservations. I plan on finding a hotel when I get there."

"Sir, we can't let you into our country if we don't have an address of where you are staying."

"So I need to make hotel reservations before I enter your country?"

"Sir, we need an address."

"I understand. I can only give you an address if I made a reservation. Are hotel reservations normally a part of your immigration procedures?"

She places my paperwork and passport in a drawer.

"Please have a seat over there, sir."

Shit, my snarky replies must have pissed her off. Fifteen long minutes pass. She stomps on my passport with that sweet visa stamp. It is the most satisfying sound I hear at a border crossing. I continue to customs where I import Jenny. She has to be sprayed with pesticides, but I think it's just a way for them to collect four dollars from me.

It's not long before I stop for gas. I ask the attendant where I can find a good place to snorkel, and he says Placencia is nice. Turns out the other guys filling up are headed there as well. The directions are simple and they say it's only two hours away so I take their advice. I wind through banana plantations and appreciate the smooth roads.

The bridge up ahead is gone, but a wooden one is nearby. It's like a railroad but the ties are a few inches apart and the rail is a foot wide. The wooden rail feels like it would be walking a tightrope, so I point Jenny towards the middle. My front wheel hits the bridge and I look down. I can see right through and it feels like I am floating on air. I freak out and cut Jenny to the right to get on the rail, but the front tire loses traction on the edge of the plank. I slide to a stop with my boot caught between Jenny and the bridge.

"God DAMN IT!"

My ankle is pinned and I can't reach Jenny to push her off.

"God FUCKING damn it!"

I grab onto a piece of the bridge and try and pull myself free but my ankle doesn't budge.

"SHIT BITCH FUCK!"

In the middle of our couple's spat the men from the gas station catch up to me and rush to my aid.

"Are you ok?" their faces drenched with worry.

"Yea I'm fine, I'm just stuck. Can you lift the bike?"

The guy hastily lifts the rear wheel and starts pulling. My leg is now a fulcrum with all of the weight of Jenny on it.

"Ah! No! No! STOP! Just stand the bike up."

They free me and the question comes again.

"Are you ok?"

There are trucks lining up waiting for this stupid gringo to get out of the way.

"I don't know, let me get across and see."

I strip off my suit and inspect my leg. There's a small bruise on my shin. It looks innocent but the slightest touch hurts like hell. There is a dull pain when I put my weight on it and that worries me more. I think I may have fractured something. I give one strong yank on my boot laces to keep a lot of pressure on it and imagine the beach paradise that awaits me 50 miles down the road.

---

I reach the southernmost tip of Placencia where there's a bunch of guys hanging out on a bench nearby.

"Where's the beach?" I ask.
"You're on da beach man, everywhere is the beach!" a man jokes.

The heat is radiating off the pavement and sweat is dripping out of the cuffs of my suit when I lower my arms. I'm not in the mood for geological jokes right now.

I find a narrow strip of beach to explore for camping spots. The sand is soft so I charge Jenny into it, speed is the key, but she just sinks. I ask around for places to camp. The only place around is behind an art gallery where a woman used to offer spots for camping. She says she has no accommodations, but all I need is a piece of ground. It's a two minute walk to the ocean. Perfect.

I am 16 degrees above the equator and Ushuaia is 55 degrees south of it. Here I am making another detour from it so I could swim in warm clear waters. I enjoy it immensely. It's my first time snorkeling. I regularly choke on salt water and freak out when the turtle grass touches my skin, but I can't get enough of it.

Out of the water I feel like I am wasting time. I've got itchy feet and just want to go south, but I've convinced myself to take advantage of the small slice of paradise and try to relax.

I extend my stay to have a proper Thanksgiving dinner at a local restaurant that I don't enjoy. I feel like a tourist and I'm hating myself and the things around me. I'm in a bad place mentally.

I spend my last evening packing up so I can get the hell out of this Corona commercial at sunrise. In the morning I realize my water backpack was stolen and I lose my shit. I use that thing every day and it saves me from dehydration, while I'm packed into my protective suit in the 90 degree heat.

Kelvin comes by while I am well into my temper tantrum. He's an 18 year old boy you would mistake for 14. We've talked over the past few days. He usually sits and watches me do whatever it is I'm doing. I'm stomping around, packing up my tent and belongings.

"What's wrong?" Kelvin asks.

"Someone stole my water pack."

"When?"

"I don't fucking know."

I make eye contact for the first time. Kelvin sits there, silent. For a half hour he just sits and watches me. Just when I thought I had no more anger, I find some.

"So are you just going to just sit there and watch me?"

He stares back at me.

"You're going to go with the staring route?"

We're having a staring contest now.

"That's all you're bringing to the table, just looking at me?"

After a minute he breaks eye contact.

"Ha! I win!"

Fifteen minutes pass and he is still there staring at me.

"How was your Thanksgiving, Kelvin?"

No response.

"How was your weekend, Kelvin?"

Still nothing.

"Why are you here?"

He looks up.

"You're not much for conversation are you?"

He looks down.

"Can you go away if all you are going to do is sit and stare?"

Nothing.

"Alright then."

Jenny is packed and ready. I ride away and Kelvin walks away. Secretly I think Kelvin's silence is a sign of guilt for stealing my stuff, but who knows? I'm riding angry, catch my luggage on a pole and Jenny falls over. Kelvin walks over to help, but I have her up before he can.

"Never mind I got it, thanks though."

Nothing.

"Again with this?"

I put my helmet on and he walks away. I hop on Jenny and before riding away I have a weird impulse. Kelvin is 100 feet away and at the top of my lungs I shout,

"KELVIN!"

I scare him and he flips around.

"HAVE A NICE DAY!"

I win another staring contest, then ride off.

---

My tourist days come to an end and it's about getting to Panama now. Things between Amber and I are better and she is meeting me there in three weeks. I've been drifting for the previous two months and it feels good to have a goal, even better that it's Amber. Ushuaia has been my goal this whole time, but it disappears behind the vibrant foreground of daily life on the move.

There is no southern border crossing in Belize so I backtrack the way I came into Guatemala. It's getting dark and I need to find a place to camp. I am close to the abandoned cattle ranch I slept at last week and I go out in search of it. I stop half a dozen times to look through the digital breadcrumbs on my GPS. It's the only way I'll find it now that it's well past dusk.

I pass through a town that has spilled out into the streets for a wedding celebration. I fantasize about crashing the party, but I'm too tired to make it a reality. I am way off course and keep heading south until I find something.

A hotel pops up a half hour down the road and I reluctantly pay the $20 for the night. I'm such a cheap-ass now-a-days. I'd sleep like a stone in a ditch or in a 5 star hotel. It makes no difference to me. I pull Jenny into the back to secure her for the night. I find two other KLRs parked, other occupants. They are newer models, by almost ten years with Arizona plates, but there's no sign of my fellow travelers around.

I should shower. It's been more than a week, but I don't want to. To just lie down is enough. I do need to eat. Bread, pastries and salami is an average dinner. I've rigged up a bread bag on the top of my luggage so it doesn't get squashed. If I leave it half empty, the remainder of the bread often rattles to crumbs. I gather a fist full and force it back together as if I was kneading dough. The crumbs absorbs all my saliva and I help it along with a few swigs of beer. I repeat until full or tipsy, whichever comes first.

I hear the other KLR owners outside. I sheepishly creep out my door. It's not often I have coherent conversations with people, let alone with fellow travelers. The father and son are examining my bike, just the way I did theirs. We acquaint ourselves with each of our machines, and finally we introduce ourselves. Bill and Bill, the two are. Three Bills and three KLRs. They have Arizona plates too, and it turns out they are from Alaska. The coincidences are amusing, but are glossed over quickly in the prospect for beer.

Big Bill is in his 40s, Little Bill is 18 and I'm in the "just right" middle at 28. Mary is our Goldilocks for the evening, Big Bill's girlfriend. She has a strong motherly quality about her and is very sweet. They are traveling to Costa Rica where Big Bill now lives.

The smallest quantity of beer you can get is a liter. My alcohol tolerance has increased since traveling, but at 125 pounds having "just one more" at these sizes can turn me into a staggering black out drunk.

We swap war stories from the road. Big Bill has learned some tricks. When ticketed, legitimately or not, Bill hands over his driver's license to the officer. He will have to return to the station with the money for the fine to get it back. What the officers don't know is that Bill has seven drivers licenses and no intention of returning to the station. I wish I had thought of "losing" my license a few times before this trip.

Little Bill works on fishing boats, taking after Big Bill. I ask if the work is similar to a TV show that documents Alaskan crab fishermen. They groan and roll their eyes. They must get this a lot.

Big Bill bursts in, "It's exactly like that, except we're not likes those pussies on TV."

Little Big corroborates, "Yea, those faggots."

Looks like I touched a nerve. I chug down the last of my first liter as Mary walks back to the table with our second round. The conversation turns towards me and my story.

"I'm heading to Ushuaia."
"All by yourself?" Big Bill asks.
"Yep."

I don't have to explain why I am going where I'm going. Big Bill has traveled and knows the destination is often the least important part of a journey. Little Bill shakes his head back and forth.

"I'd never be out here alone without a gun," he says.
"When it comes to fight or flight, I am on the far edge of the flight spectrum. I don't think a gun would do me much good."
"Carrying a gun can get you in a lot of trouble," says Big Bill.
Finally some sensibility.
He continues, "Besides, I'm pretty good with a knife after 20 years on a fishing boat. I can gut a human just as easily as a fish with a sharp enough knife."

He makes a zig-zag-zig motion across my belly and both Bills erupt into laughter.

"I hope all this talk doesn't make you nervous," Big Bill says apologetically.
"Nah, it's fine."

Secretly I am thankful for the fact that our meals don't need silverware.

It disturbs me that Little Bill thinks that he would need a gun for protection in Central America. For those who haven't been, it is natural to think of these places as lawless cesspools of violence. This is what I used to think. Then I turned off my TV, ignored everyone who's never been and listened to those who have. Everyone has been so nice. When I've been in need people have always been eager to help. Perhaps his experiences have differed from mine, or his presuppositions are harder to break.

I play catch up with my beer as Mary brings our third round to the table. I want to make it to Guatemala City tomorrow. I am already drunk so I forget about the 300 miles ahead of me when our bottles clink for a cheers.

The next morning I wake up confused at the sight of a new ceiling. It takes me a few moments to realize where the hell I am.

"You're in Guatemala Bill."

Then I wonder where in Guatemala.

"In Quetzaltenango. No, just south of Tikal, or maybe Lacacion."

Most mornings I have to look at my GPS to know where I am. Sometimes I enjoy not knowing. It matters less than you think. There are only a couple arteries that allow you to go south. With the help of 24 satellites and this GPS in my hand, I know where I am on this Earth within a couple meters of precision. Yet all I need to know is, if I'm riding with the sun on my left shoulder, I'm going the right way. Sometimes I don't know where I am, but anywhere pointed south is right. I never knew aimlessness could feel so good.

I hope to cover a lot of miles today. I leave the dirt mountain roads with their switchbacks taking me up, down and around. A black band in the distance draws near and I eat up the miles. I am in a very calm state, almost meditative. I swerve through the cars and potholes effortlessly. It's all reflex now. I'm not thinking about anything. I am motionless and it feels like it's the ground that's moving under my wheels, not me. I am here, right now, but sometimes I double check my GPS to confirm where "here" is.

I decide to try and keep riding until I reach 100 miles on my trip meter. It's a gauge for when I should consider finding fuel and keeps my butt in the saddle longer to prevent dilly dallying. I pass by a gas station. The dial reads 97 and I'm not in the mood to round up to

100. There will be another station somewhere. If not I'll run out of gas and there will be some way to get more.

By the end of the day I've logged 300 miles. I feel like I could do another, but the light is fading. Tomorrow I will make another big push for Antigua via Guatemala City. Everyone has nothing but good things to say about it. I stop in a small town for the night. After a long day of riding, walking feels foreign. My identity is melding with Jenny's and I clomp around the town like a toddler in oversized boots.

---

When I crossed the border in Mexico I saw a sign that read, "Mexico" with an arrow. It referred to the capital, Mexico City. The same is true in Guatemala. For the last thousand miles I've been seeing arrows for "Guatemala" and each time I do a double-take. Borders are just an imaginary line and I want to make sure I haven't crossed into another country accidentally.

Back home I noticed that when a man from Latin America gets angry people attribute it to his fiery Latin blood. This principle is also true for traffic in Latin America. The traffic isn't "crazy", "dangerous" or "insane". It's a combination of many things including these, but in my mind it's simply "Latin." I am 30 miles from the center of Guatemala City and the traffic is getting more Latin than usual. I'm on a freeway and trying to find the exit ramp to Antigua. I follow the signs, but I end up running in circles for an hour. It is hot today and I need to keep a breeze flowing through the vents in my suit otherwise I'll overheat.

I find a route leading to El Salvador and take it instead of going to Antigua. This is a luxury you don't often get while traveling with others. No pulling off to the side of the road to discuss a game plan. No planning at all if you don't want. Just ride with your impulses. I never used to have impulses. Maybe they were always there and were overshadowed by my meticulous planning. I'm not thinking as much, and for me this is a good thing.

I ride just shy of the El Salvador border. My excitement to see Amber in Panama grows. Tomorrow I will be one country closer to her. I've been on the road for 97 days, living out my dream while she sits at home. Things have been hard between us and I've hurt her a lot. I am preoccupied with finding food, fuel, shelter and riding. My empathy has decreased over the months. I'm alone in my own world and it's hard to see the effects of my actions on anyone else. Seeing her in Panama is going to burst this bubble I've built. My excitement is mixed with anxiety. She won't be an abstraction in the form of an email, or a phone call anymore. I am elated to see her, but it comes with the reality of all the pain I've caused her over these months. In Panama I'll be forced to witness an ugly part of myself I'm usually really good at ignoring.

I reach the border for El Salvador. I exit Guatemala with ease and enter the limbo zone. The perimeter of this zone is between countries and is ruled by the immigration regulations. Not going mad here is a test in patience and a bit of detective work as well. I get my visa without a problem. Just have to import Jenny and I am off to a new country. It's 11:30 A.M. and I approach the counter. I feel small in the face of the staff. My fate is at their whim and their attitude is that of disinterested baristas. The man says he will be with me in a moment. I want to sit, but I stay standing at the counter, making my existence known. With his back to me I watch the man check his watch and ruffle through papers in his suitcase. He scratches off numbers on a lotto ticket. He examines it carefully and calls the number on it. He is packing up all his belongings. Did he win? He is keeping his cool if he did. No one answers his call. Who knows if he even dialed a valid number. At noon a co-worker takes over his shift. She gets me through in five minutes. Lesson of the day: never attempt a border crossing around lunchtime.

I hug the coastline and it feels like I am back in California. I get glimpses of the vast blue carpet through the few clearings in the trees. Whenever I took the coastal road in California I was headed north and the ocean was to my left. Now, with it to my right, there's no delusion of where I am and where I'm headed. I keep picturing the South American continent and it scares the hell out me. I'll reach the halfway point at the five month mark, and I plan on being on the road for eight months. That leaves me with three months to finish the second half, and doubts over the feasibility of my plan consume me. I focus on what I can manage to do in the next week and ignore the rest until I get there.

---

This journey fell in my Ray LaMontagne year. Ray is an American folk singer I discovered six months ago. If you asked me what music I like, I'd answer, "Ray LaMontagne." If you asked what else I like, I'd answer with a history of what I've listened to and it would round out to about one artist a year. Like counting backwards it's easy for me to recall what artist came before the other and ultimately I always end with Pearl Jam back in grammar school.

I listen to music while I ride. It accents the experience and I can't ride without it very often. Last year's band was mostly instrumental and when there were vocals, it was a made up language, dubbed, "Hopelandic", by the band, Sigur Ros. Throughout the lonely deserts of the southwest, I was taken to euphoric highs and somber lows with the same album or song on repeat for hours. Ray's music is saturated with poetry and I spend a lot of time analyzing the lyrics and finding meaning in a chorus or a rhyme. This is new for me and takes the abstraction out of my previous listening habits. I wonder who I will be listening to at the end of this journey.

I am blasting through the coastal road and getting into a groove. Jenny is falling into the curves perfectly. My finger is on the pulse of the road and I'm finding its rhythm. I round every corner effortlessly, without a thought in my mind. I don't noticed the music blasting in my ears until Ray chimes in:

"Is your hometown bringing ya down?"

Weight distribution on a motorcycle is key for stabilization, and influencing that stability is often done through the foot pegs. The music takes over and my boots stomp on Jenny's pegs to the beat. Ray goes on:

"Are you gonna step in line, like your Daddy done?
Punch in the time and climbing life's long ladder."

A conversation with an old friend comes to mind. He was very concerned with my plans for traveling and we argued over it a lot.

"Is this it?" I asked, gesturing at everything in whatever shit bar we happened to be in.
"Do we just work until we die?"
"Yes!" he replied emphatically.

We shared the same cynicism among many areas in life, but this was an alley I couldn't walk down with him. The end of the song coincides with the sight of a roadside restaurant. I've been having too much fun riding and I finally stop for an overdue lunch. The ocean side view makes me want to hang my hammock and watch the sunset. I crack open a beer and take in my surroundings. I picture my friend back home in front of his TV and can't help but think, "He's doing it wrong".

I start looking for places to stay for the evening. I pass by fancy beachside resorts, but I just want a deserted place to pitch my tent. Spots on the beach are hard to come by, so I check out the rates at a hotel. It's $25 for the night so I ask if I can camp in their parking lot. They don't budge on the price. I backtrack to a small town I passed earlier and make my way through a series of makeshift shacks and huts. Jenny and I put-put through the neighborhood and kids run out to see who's making all the racket.

At the end of the road I find an old man in a shack with plenty of room for Jenny and me. I ask if I can camp for the night for $10 and he readily accepts. He points to the back, exposed to the ocean, perfect. We seal the deal with a handshake and I realize he has only one eye. I'm weirded out by it, but I try not to show it. We're still shaking hands as we chat. He assures me everything will be ok here and I believe him. There are points where we don't understand each other, but we are still shaking hands. The confusion continues and he finally releases his grip. He points to his empty socket to indicate that he will watch over my belongings. I'm not sure if he's trying to make a joke, so I do my best to contain the laughter bubbling up inside me.

I take Jenny inside and hang my hammock. The sand is a soft black powder, almost like ashes. Now to fetch dinner. There's only a couple hundred people living here and I didn't see much on the way in. The streets are sand packed tight and I clomp down them looking for a restaurant. Some places look like the dinner table of a private home, and I don't have the nerve to approach. I walk the length of the street and a guy lures me in speaking English. He doesn't bother speaking Spanish with this gringo.

The place is in the open air like all the rest, with a meager roof that would barely stop the slowest drizzle. The tablecloths are orange and yellow checkerboard. This reminds me of a psychological study showing that this mixture of colors is subconsciously unsettling to people. It's subtle, but strong enough to keep people from loitering at the local burger joint whose walls are striped with the dizzying pattern. The place is empty except for me so maybe there is something to the theory. A female dog lies against the wall with a half dozen puppies suckling at her teats. This weirds me out more than the clashing colors of the table cloth.

There's no menu, just Lucas, and he sits down.

"What would you like?" he asks.

"Just a beer and some food."

"We have chicken and beef."

I let him surprise me with the food. He didn't say what "beef" or "chicken" means so it's a crap shoot anyways.

He barks orders to the ladies in the kitchen, presumably his wife and mother, then brings back two beers, one for me and one for him.

"Where are you going? Where are you from?" he asks.

I've heard this question a hundred times and it always follows the same order. I'm always perplexed by the first question. I am going to Argentina, but when I answer with this, it's so far away it causes confusion. This happened in America too, so it's not an issue of language. Sometimes I answer, "South America" but ultimately people ask where in South America and it leads to Argentina and Ushuaia. It's a simple question that I complicate. So I narrow my destination.

"I'm headed to Panama."

The second question raises confusion in my own mind instead of the other person's. I lived in Phoenix for three years, and ultimately started there, but I grew up in Chicago and lived there the longest. I have Arizona plates and I feel like I will get caught in a lie that's not really a lie.

"I'm from Chicago."

Lucas and the rest of Latin America says "Chicago" just the way I love to hear it.

"Ah Chee-ka-go, I used to live there", he says.
"Oh really?"
"Yea I was a truck driver for five years, then I got into an accident. They revoked my visa and said, word for word, 'Go back to your fucking country.'"

If he's making this up, he's done his homework, since this sums up exactly what someone from Chicago would say.

My food arrives and whatever it is, it's delicious, and I finish after two liters of beer. I stumble out and pass a pit bull that looks similar to a friend's back home. I bend down to pet the guy and he growls. I don't take the warning seriously and kneel down to extend my hand for him to smell. He bites it, and I stumble off laughing. Lucas runs to see if I am ok. He didn't break the skin, but it still hurt like a bitch. He apologizes and I dismiss it since it was my fault. I ask if he has rabies and he assures me he's fine. I pencil, "google rabies symptoms" in my notebook as I walk back to my camp.

I want to walk across the shore, but the tide came in fast. It is pitch black except for the moonlight. The waves crash on the sand with a force I've never witnessed before. I wonder how they will feel so I strip down to my underwear to find out. Drunken night swimming, a winning combination.

The water rushes over my feet, ice cold. It's not long before the waves are knocking me over. They are too tall for me to jump over so I dive into them. They hit me like a punch to the face. I tumble end over end on every axis. I laugh hysterically in between choking on the salt water that forced itself through my nostrils. After a half hour I am exhausted. This foolish battle was really fun losing. I look around and pause for a moment to take in what's happening. I'm pissed drunk on a Salvadoran beach nursing a dog bite and sleeping near the chicken coop of a one eyed man's house. Good day.

I pass through the capital, San Jose, and stumble upon a Kawasaki shop to get an oil change. I am sorely in need of a front tire too. It should have been replaced 2,000 miles ago. I want to replace it before I reach Amber in Panama since she will be riding with me. I put myself at a higher risk. Crashing is no big deal anymore to me, but I'd hate to have Amber get hurt.

I push on to San Miguel to set myself up for a crossing into Honduras tomorrow. Whenever I arrive in a city I head for the highest church steeple. It's always in the central town square and there's always a bank close to god's house so I can hit the ATM. The cities have become noisier as I get further south. I thought I would get used to it but I haven't. The honking car horns and the blasting music is too much for me. I chase an anti-anxiety pill with a swig of beer before I go for my evening walk.

There isn't much to the town. Big dots on the map raise my expectations, but everything is closed by six o'clock, something I haven't seen very often before. I walk by sagging breasts attached to an old woman and covered by a shirt that reads "Girls Gone Wild" and I pray she doesn't get the urge to do so.

# DAY 101
# AMATILLO, HONDURAS

"Be kind,
for everyone you meet is fighting a harder battle."

Plato

Latitude:    013° 35' 50" N
Longitude: 087° 45' 59" W

11,379 miles to Ushuaia

---

Within a mile of the Honduras border people are running into the road and flagging me down. They are civilians and I don't know what they want, but I don't stop to find out. Exiting El Salvador is easy, but the Honduran side is another story.

All the countries so far have had a lack of development, and this isn't something I would consider bad, but the conditions of this border are testing me greatly. There is a general disorder to everything and people swarm around me. I repeat over and over, "go away, let me think."

A helper convinces me to let him assist me through the border crossing procedure for a small fee. I don't know what currency is used or the exchange rate. I find a money changer and get some lempiras. It is ten o'clock in the morning and my helper assures me he can get me through the border before lunch at noon. He wants to take my papers and get the job finished, but I insist on being aware of every step along the way. We go to a copy shop since everything has to be in triplicates. Copies of the stamped copies needed to be copied in triplicate too. We wander from one building to the next. I can't keep up, and my helper isn't slowing down for me. On the last step of the process I give in and relax in the shade. I'm in limbo zone with some guy running around with my identity.

Two other motorcyclists pull up next to me. One from New York and the other from England. They are riding to Ushuaia like me and look worried about the state of the border conditions.

"It's a bit complicated, more complicated than any previous crossing I've done. I'd recommend a helper. I've got one doing all the leg work," I tell them.

My helper appears from nowhere. He shouts my name, and starts running the opposite direction. I follow him to sign whatever he tells me to sign, wondering if I'm the owner of a Honduran timeshare now.

"Almost done William!" and he disappears into another building.

I wait some more and swap stories with the other riders. Their helpers call them away to do the same dance I am finishing. I chuckle to myself at their confusion, as if I hadn't been confused like them only an hour ago. Some people try on the New York rider's helmet. I don't like people messing with other people's things, so I take it away and rest it on his the mirror of his brand new KLR650. Ten minutes later the bike falls over for no reason, and I can't help but think I am responsible. The New York guy is pissed.

"Can't be the first time, right? It's another battle scar."
"First time actually," he fires back.

All this time without a fall. I find this strange, but if he knew my record I'm sure he'd think the same about me.

My helper is back, "William! Come! Come!"

He hops in a motorcycle cab and rides to the border checkpoint. I scramble my gear together and say a quick goodbye to New York and England.

"Good luck fellas, maybe I'll see ya down the road."

It's 11:50 AM and in ten minutes the border will grind to a halt for lunch. They are going to be here for a while.

I meet my helper at the border and everything is all set, just seven more dollars for fumigation. The fumigation guy is already packing up for lunch and can't be bothered. He stamps a ticket indicating Jenny has been sterilized and waves me on. The agreed upon five dollars for my helper's service turns into ten. I give him seven and he speeds back to save another soul in border crossing limbo.

An hour down the road I'm stopped at a checkpoint. My luggage doesn't have reflective stickers, and I incur a two dollar "fine." I am in a hurry to make it to Nicaragua before dusk and I don't care to fight so I pay the man. Later I fill up at a gas station. The meter indicates four dollars of gas and I pay the attendant accordingly. He says I need to pay double what the meter says. I'm trying to convert lempiras to dollars, and liters to gallons to get a sense of how much that is. I argue with him and ask why I have to pay double. Why don't I pay what the meter says? We get nowhere. I only have eight dollars left and I reluctantly give it to him. He's satisfied and I ride off. I feel like I keep getting screwed left and right, and I'm dedicated to getting out of Honduras. I don't want to give this country another dollar and I don't want to spend the night here. I picture my own version of Central America's anatomy. Mexico is the tailbone, Panama a penis and Honduras is the asshole.

I blast across the country. The roads are a minefield of potholes, but I keep my speed up and swerve through them just the same. This takes my mind off things and I stop riding angry. Police checkpoints consist of a couple cops sitting under a tree picking who they want to stop and gringos on motorcycles are good targets. I cringe when I see them in the distance.

"Please don't stop me.

Please don't stop me.

Please don't stop me."

I pass, give a big sigh of relief and continue as if they never existed, but soon enough another one pops up.

"Please don't stop me.

Please don't stop me.

Please don't stop me."

A subtle but forceful flick of the wrist signals me to stop. I stop in the middle of the road and keep the engine running to create a scene with cars stopping behind me. They tell me to pull off to the side of the road, but I only move Jenny over a foot. This repeats four times before I clear the road, but cars still crawl by. They ask for my papers and I show them. I am quiet, and I stare at them with a fierce look. They flick their wrist and I am free to go.

It's four o'clock and I make it to the border. I don't have much light left to exit Honduras and enter Nicaragua. The exit is just as confusing as the entrance. I present all my papers, they stamp away, and I am a free man. At the bridge crossing, the Honduran guard asks me for a ticket I need to pass, but I never got one. I return to the office and the man behind the counter says he gave me the ticket and I insist that he didn't. He points at my document bag, and I say it's not there. We sit and stare at each other for a moment and I realize this isn't working. Maybe I am mistaking what piece of paper they are talking about. I pull out every single paper and lay it across the counter asking if it is what they are looking for.

With each piece of paper my frustration is building. By the time I arrive at the twelfth piece I am slamming the pages down and I'm displaying that my bag is empty. He reviews my papers, and gives me the small ticket I need to pass, my freedom in the size of a fortune cookie.

I return to Jenny and try to return order to my document bag. I am smiling and relieved to get out of this country. As I compose myself I have an audience of six helpers watching me. Five of them saw me when I first arrived and the expression on my face was enough for them not to approach me. The sixth guy just came by, a kid, and he sits and spouts out a list of services he has to offer. I say no thanks a dozen times. He keeps going and now I just ignore him. There is no one else here, and he's still rambling off his list and trying to get some money out of me. Finally I snap, take a few steps towards him and bellow at a volume I never knew I was capable of:

"NOOOOOO!"

The kid shuts up. I walk back to Jenny and the other five guys are roaring with laughter at the sixth. They point at the kid, and mimic me.

"No! No! No!"

I start Jenny up and the kid starts walking toward me, mocking me as well. I smile at him and rev Jenny loud to drown him out. I give the kid the finger and peel out, accidentally doing a wheelie. I ride out of Honduras with my finger raised high, one final salute.

The Nicaraguan border is easy to cross. After an hour and a half the immigration officer reaches for the visa stamper and I hear that sweet sound in two quick successions. The first stamp on the ink pad, and the second on my passport, blotting out Guatemala. They had the whole page, why there? You think their aim would be good after doing this all day. Regardless, the final stamp at a border is like a cigarette after sex, but without the sex. Someone is getting fucked, but not the way you'd like it.

Today I exited El Salvador, entered Honduras, then exited and entered Nicaragua. I need to put at ease what is left of my battered spirit and a desolate camp site will help. I spot a ridge off the road with a slope that leads to it. I charge up the hill to find a dead end out of sight, inconspicuous enough to sleep for the night. I dismount Jenny and notice a little boy, maybe five only, walking toward me. An older man appears behind him and they stand at a distance, watching me. I scramble up the rock face to discover a small house on the opposite end of the peak. Maybe I'm on their land, or maybe they're just curious. Either way, I go down to meet the neighbors.

I greet the man with a bright smile and a handshake. He is in his 30s with sandpaper hands. I apologize for my abrupt entrance and ask if it is possible for me to camp just for the evening. The man nods with a smile and I'm grateful. He doesn't say much, but the boy is asking me all kinds of questions. I'm finally matched with a vocabulary similar to mine, and we're carrying out a coherent conversation.

It's not long before the whole family is coming up to greet me: the grandparents of the boy, his mother and two sisters. The grandmother appears to be in charge. She embraces me with a warm welcome. I introduce myself in the same way I have to strangers for months:

"I am from the United States and I am traveling to Ushuaia, Argentina."

With the sight of Jenny it's evident how I am traveling, and that one sentence explains it all. The sweet grandmother invites me to sleep under her roof with the rest of the family and I accept.

I bring Jenny and my things into their home where everyone but the grandparents sleep in hammocks. The older ones sleep on a simple bed of straw. Baby chicks wander around the dirt floor, and pigs and chickens wander around the fenceless perimeter. The grandmother is full of life and speaks so quickly I don't understand. When I apologize for the confusion she pulls my shoulder down to her five foot frame and speaks loud enough in my ear for it to hurt. I wince back, laughing and the family laughs along with me. I tell her my ears are fine, but my Spanish is poor.

I am carrying my things into the house and the grandmother ambushes me with a baby. I don't understand a word she's saying, but she's a grandmother cooing at her grandchild and that is all there is to be understood. She extends her hands to pass the child to me. My anxiety is higher in these situations than when I was threatened with jail back in Mexico. I'm not good with babies. I feel like I am going to break or drop them. These fragile little balls whose native language is emotion are intimidating. At 28 years old, I still have trouble with this language. Give me a kid with a capacity for rationality and I've got something to work with. But as the days have passed on my journey, I've been realizing more and more how overrated the mind is. I cradle the baby in my arms, notice his red hair and find myself grinning. I've known these people for only an hour and they are trusting me with their baby. I try and understand the quality of these people that evoke such generosity. It doesn't take long for me to simply accept it for what it is and stop trying to understand everything.

I setup my hammock on the tree trunks that support the woven walls of reeds. The sun has set and dusk is fading. I am entertaining for them, and once I am finished we all sit and look each other. There is nothing uncomfortable about the silence, and when my eyes make contact with a family member a smile always follows. I'm no longer a scared American interpreting their behavior with alternative menacing motives. It's dark now and with routine everyone gets ready for bed. I am exhausted and eager to collapse after such a long day.

---

The family's rooster screeches at six o'clock and an hour later I am on the road, on a mission to cover all of Nicaragua and cross into Costa Rica. Not impossible, but not easy. I am stopped at a police checkpoint and all my paperwork is in order. I am free to continue on my way, but I get the impression that if there weren't so many people around there might have been some kind of "fine."

A couple of hours later, I am stopped again. They say my insurance has expired. Either I paid $12 for only one day of insurance, or the little girl living next to a trash fire made a mistake while filling out the paperwork. The officers allow me to take care of this problem on the side of the road for $10.

Among the fantasizing of pristine beaches I replay the previous two stops in my head. I didn't notice radios on the officers. They were in the middle of nowhere. Could I have just kept going? Maybe next time I don't notice that they are signaling me to pull over. Bigger misunderstandings have happened.

Two hours later a third police checkpoint signals me to pull over. I'm never going to make it to Costa Rica with all this bull shit. There is some traffic, and I pull off to the side of the road and slow down, way down. The officer is crossing his hands waiting to see what this gringo is up to. What if I don't stop? The question in my mind is an affirmation of the action. I don't stop. I roll by them slowly, and I keep going slow. I'm not running. I'm just not stopping. If I was running I'd be speeding away, but I'm not so I'm not running. My eyes are glued to my rear view mirror and an officer waves his arm to the rest in a motion indicating that they've got a runner. There's no mistake about what is going on now.

Once the checkpoint disappears in my rearview mirror, I punch the throttle wide open. With all this traffic they can't catch me. While I split down lanes of traffic, I come to emergency stops at intersections, no telling if there might be a cop coming through. When I see the coast is clear I gun it. I'm running, but I don't want it to look like I'm running.

My adrenaline is jacked. I am fixated on the road and even a stray cat can't hide from my sight. Speed, split, stop, look, repeat. Jenny and I are one. My eyelids hang halfway open and the muscles in my face go limp. I am a Zen master and fugitive all in one, and I push out the one question that can put this insanity to rest:

"What the fuck are you doing Bill?"

I am not the kind of guy who runs from cops. But right now I'm like every one of those idiots on the news, except no helicopter. I reached my breaking point. I am sick of being jerked around. Let's see what happens. What's done is done so I keep running.

At the next intersection a cop car screeches to a halt in the middle of it. It's a red light and I stop behind the line like a good law abiding motorist. The cop launches out of his car leaving the door open. I look to the left, and to the right in a "What's all the commotion?" kind of way. My hands are on my hips. They've been chasing a runner, and I don't want to look like I might run with my hands on the throttle. The officer grabs my chest and I throw down Jenny's kickstand just before I am pulled off.

"What is happening?! I don't understand!" I shout.

I am marched to the back seat of the cop car and thrown in with my helmet still on my head. My jaw tightens and the muscles in my face spring with fear. The reality of the situation kicks in.

Officer Rodriguez is clutching my chest the whole time. He's shouting at me, and waving his finger. I can only make out bits and pieces, but I know what this is all about anyways. A street merchant asks if I need a translator through the window.

"Yes, please!" I say.

He hops in the front passenger seat and talks to Rodriguez.

The merchant says, "You are being arrested for evading the police."

Ok, no surprises there, I've got the "stupid gringo act" I can leverage. I'll be ok. We are caught in traffic as we head toward the police station in the opposite direction of the chase. A taxi driver yells at the officers, making it clear that he is happy to see me where I am. What else is he saying to them?

The merchant and Rodriguez talk and there is more news. He says I am also being arrested for attempted assault on an officer and my heart sinks. I am fucked. Still, the first question I ask myself is, "How much is this going to cost?" Probably in the thousands. Maybe I won't be making it to South America. We arrive at the station.

Rodriguez pulls me out of the car and leads me into a room, with a table, four chairs and some filing cabinets.

"Where is my motorcycle?" I ask.

He doesn't answer, but minutes later I hear her exhaust. At least she is ok. Who knows what will happen to me. Rodriguez is pointing at me with the same grimace and saying I am in big trouble. I play the dumb gringo.

"Why? I don't understand."

Officer Garcia walks in and starts going through my paperwork. He is less high-strung than Rodriguez and he knows a little English. Garcia finds notes from my Spanish lessons in Guatemala.

"So you say you don't speak Spanish?" he asks with a smirk.
"Just a little," I admit.

He glares at me and returns to my paperwork.

Rodriguez and a new officer, Lopez, lead me to Jenny and tell me to start unpacking. Lopez is laughing and joking around with me. He makes funny faces behind Rodriguez's grimace as he talks to me, and I laugh. The tension is lowering, until I wonder what they will make of the four month supply of medication I have stashed in my bags. How do I explain that? Maybe they think it's drugs. That's what they are looking for. Why else would I run?

Rodriguez is going through everything. He is inspecting the inside of my chapstick and toothpaste. He asks me to open up a big plastic tube on my bike where I keep all my tools. I can only open it using my hand axe. I slowly reach for the axe.

"Can I?" I ask sheepishly.

He watches me closely as I loosen the opening of the tube. I slowly place the axe on the ground and he kicks it out of my reach. I pull out a wrench, and point to it.

"Just tools," I say.

We methodically move through all my bags and reach what I fear the most: my stash of anti-depression and anxiety pills.

"What is this?" asks Rodriguez.
"It's medication for my head, a four month supply." I say.

He tosses the pills on the ground with the rest of my belongings and we go back into the station.

Garcia has made copies of all my documents and is making notes. He is going through my computer now and I can hear him opening up video logs from the road. Rodriguez is going through the videos on my camera. At this point four new officers gathered around to see the show. Moans and screams comes from my laptop and Garcia looks up at me. How did he find my porn folder so quickly?

"You know pornography is illegal" he says, with a stone cold expression.
"Are you fucking serious?!"
He smirks, "No man. It's a fucking joke!"

It's silent as everyone is shuffling through my belongings. I take a moment to gather the words in Spanish:

"If I thought I needed to stop, I would have. I didn't think I needed to stop, so I didn't."

I kept repeating this, five or six times until I start annoying Rodriguez. I sit, waiting for what's next until I hear Garcia and Lopez talking.

"Gringo es famoso," Garcia says to Lopez.
"En Mexico?" Lopez asks.
I interrupt, "do you know me from the newspapers in Mexico?"

Garcia nods. I impulsively smile from the fame factor, then realize it is derived from getting Mexican cops fired. Is this good or bad for me? I keep quiet. One of the officers asks if I was videotaping them. I smirk, look around the room, and pause for a moment before I answer.

I flash a quick nod and the room erupts into laughter. I feel like everything is going to be ok. I laugh along with them and secretly hope they don't ask to see the footage I never actually shot.

I'm getting antsy. What happens next? I'm resigned. If I have to spend a few days in jail, let's get them started. Lopez takes his cuffs out and clinks them together. I stand up and put my hands behind my back facing him. Is this the next step? On with it then. He puts the cuffs away like the joker Lopez is. It's only been two hours, but I've gotten close to these guys in that captive/captor kind of way.

Garcia is gathering my papers. What happens next? The suspense is killing me. He pushes my bag of documents across the table and gives me a stern warning about stopping for the police. I realize I am walking out of here in a couple of minutes and relief washes over me.

Garcia adds, "Next time, you get a ticket!"

I struggle to contain the laughter and humbly nod in understanding. I got a "ticket" from a guy four hours ago for bad insurance papers, and here I ran from the cops and walk out without paying a dime.

The arrest only ate up a few hours of my time so I still have a chance to make it to Costa Rica. No fucking around though. Stop at stop signs, obey the speed limit and no passing on solid yellows.

An hour later on a long straight away I am passing a slow heavy truck on a solid yellow line. It's impossible to obey the laws here, at least for me. As I pass the truck I see an officer in the shade of a tree with a radar detector. I wasn't speeding, but he's got me on crossing a solid yellow. He motions me to pull over, and this time I do.

I give him my International Drivers License because it's disposable identification. He tells me I crossed on a solid yellow line.

"That truck was so slow! There were no other cars around!" I argue.

He is writing up a ticket for $150. I tell him I don't have enough, and that a friend is up ahead where we are supposed to meet. If he takes my identification I will return to the station to pay the fine and retrieve it. I have no intention of doing either. The officer's bargaining powers diminish and I can see it in his eyes. He writes $40 on his hand and says we can just take care of it here. I open my wallet to reveal eight dollars and tell him it's all I have. He takes it, and I am free to go. I am getting better at this.

I stop at a bank to get some "ticket" cash to get through the rest of the country. An elderly man approaches me, accompanied by his son who speaks some English. The young man is translating and telling me that his father saw me in the newspapers and would like to thank me for fighting the corrupt police.

"Que bueno! Que bueno!" the old man repeats as he shakes my hand.

The news must have spread further south than I thought. I'm a hero in this man's eyes, but I might be a target for others. There's not much I can do. I keep riding, at least I'll be a moving target.

---

I cross Nicaragua with two hours of daylight to spare. I spend the last of my córdobas and exit the country into the limbo zone with Costa Rica in eye sight. Honduras bled me dry of dollars and I am under the impression that if Nicaragua had cash machines, surely the Costa Rica side would as well. I learn another border crossing lesson: always have cash. American dollars are the best to have. You get a crappy exchange rate from the money changers on the sidewalk, but border fees typically don't exceed 20 dollars. I need ten dollars to import Jenny. No big deal, I'll just head back to the Nicaraguan side and pull some córdobas to change into dollars, which in turn will be changed into Costa Rican colónes.

I turn back to the ATM in Nicaragua, but I'm stopped by the border guard. I had just seen him a few minutes ago and he remembers me.

"There's no ATMs on the Costa Rica side. Can I stop back at your immigration office to get some cash?" I ask.

"You can't pass back into Nicaragua without proof that you've exited Costa Rica."

"I haven't entered Costa Rica and I need cash to do so."

He doesn't care about the deadlock I find myself in.

"The building is just right over there. I don't want to formally re-enter Nicaragua. I just need to use the ATM so I can enter Costa Rica."

"You can't enter Nicaragua without paperwork proving you've exited Costa Rica" he says.

"I can't even enter Costa Rica to exit it!"

We are spinning in circles and I'm not getting anywhere.

"Can I leave my motorcycle here while I walk over to the building? I am not going anywhere without it."

"Sorry sir."

I take out a piece of paper and start drawing on it. I learned this tactic from the Mexican cops that tried to tell me I was going to jail if I didn't give them $500. I draw two lines down the paper to form three columns. I write "Nicaragua" in the left column and "Costa Rica" in the right. The center column has a large question mark.

"We are here," pointing at the question mark, the border limbo zone between countries, "I can't enter Costa Rica without returning to Nicaragua, but you are telling me I can't enter Nicaragua without first entering Costa Rica, which is impossible without entering Nicaragua." I am drawing arrows all over the page to try and communicate this concept to him. I can see I am getting through to him. "If I can't access the ATM I will be here forever." I point to the question mark. He tells me to leave my motorcycle and I am free to re-enter Nicaragua.

There is no cash in the ATM. A guard says someone is on their way to re-fill it. The Costa Rica immigration offices will be closing soon. All I can do is wait, and I scope out potential camping spots in my limbo zone should the offices close. I've never been so relieved to see men with shotguns walk towards me. I'm leaning against the ATM and they are here to refill it. I get the cash and enter Costa Rica just before the border closes.

I have no clue where I am going and the light is fading quick. I pick an arbitrary road that dead ends on the coast according to my GPS. An hour later I find a deserted spot and hang my hammock. I haven't eaten all day. There was no time for it. I was so stressed out I didn't have an appetite anyways. I cook a cup of rice and don't bother with spices. Anything is delicious when you are hungry enough.

It's morning and I head to Playa Negra. There's a small restaurant with cold beer and a dozen surfers. I wrestle Jenny on the soft sand to make camp under some trees. There's sweat collecting in the cuffs of my sleeves by the time I get Jenny over to the right spot. I rip off my suit and run for the water. The waves are pounding down on me and once I can no longer touch the bottom a big one tosses me around on every axis. I return to Jenny still coughing up salt water and laughing at myself. Nearby families are laughing at me too.

I decide to stay here for a couple of days to rest. I nap, drink and eat. Surfers catch waves of the aquatic kind while I am behind my laptop trying to catch weak radio waves from a distant wireless router. I've been offline for the past few days and it's nice to catch up.

After a couple of days at Playa Negra I move onto Playa del Coco where there is supposed to be good snorkeling. I rent some gear and swim along the edge of a rocky shore. There's puffer fish all over and I chase them to try and get them to puff up with no luck. The town is larger than I imaged and the spots to stealth camp are sparse. I'm too cheap to pay $10 for a room so I camp in some brush along the beach. I come back from snorkeling to find my motorcycle gloves have been stolen from my tent. I notice some dents on Jenny's gas tank too. Most of them are from me, but there are some fresh ones that are deeper. It's no big deal to me, this is why I don't like nice things. It's something to get pissed about when it gets damaged. The random vandalism worries me and I wonder if I am safe camping on the beach here.

It's dark and I'm reading in my tent. A flashlight shines on my campsite a couple times. It freaks me out so I follow the guy to see what's going on. It's probably nothing, but I won't rest until I find out. He lives nearby and noticed my tent. He is checking up on me and tells me that I've picked a very dangerous area to sleep. I didn't take the hint from the theft and the vandalism, but I'd be stupid not to listen to someone who knows the area. I pack up and find a hostel to crash at for the night.

I can understand the theft, but the vandalism bothers me. Why would someone do such a thing? I try not to dwell on it. Lesson learned: ask the locals before stealth camping in populated areas.

Amber is landing in Panama City in ten days. I'm excited to see her, and it puts a fire under my ass. I can't be a beach bum forever.

# DAY 107
# SAN JOSÉ, COSTA RICA

"The human brain is a complex organ with the wonderful power of enabling man to find reasons for continuing to believe whatever it is that he wants to believe."

Voltaire

Latitude:    009° 55' 37" N
Longitude: 084° 04' 55" W

10,757 miles to Ushuaia

---

I'm not fond of big cities, anywhere really. They are loud, busy and expensive. It had been weeks since I stayed in one so I decide to check out San Jose, the capital of Costa Rica. It is like most major cities in Latin America. Colorful, and bustling, but a little grimier than most. It is getting dark and I am trying to find the location of my couch surfing host. He didn't give me an address through the previous weeks' worth of correspondence, just a series of directions from landmarks:

> "Three blocks past the grocery store, can't miss it, then take a sharp right around the bar next to the bodega, and I'm the pink one story house."
> "How do you get mail?" I ask.
> "I asks senders to write these very instructions on the envelope," he says.

I miss the grocery store you can't miss, then I pick and choose from the numerous bodegas and bars. I find the street with a layer of chipped and fading pink paint on the house.

The front gate is shut, and I can't reach the doorbell. There's a faint hint that someone might be home, but it might just be a kitchen light left on. I beep my horn a couple times and feel bad about disturbing the neighbors. However, if things got quiet people might start to think something was wrong. Silences is rare here. I see movement in a window, but they don't respond to my beeping. Like a teenager trying not to wake up the parents of a girl I'm courting, I throw rocks at the window. The figure starts moving through the house, and lights are turning on and off. My taps at the window and horn honking don't get their attention. I point my bike towards the window and when the figure moves into the living room I start flicking my high beams on and off. He answers the door to see what the light show outside is all about.

The figure is a pale blond Frenchman. Orlando, who I made arrangements with, is not home. The Frenchman is draped in a robe so loose I know his briefs are green, and a couple sizes too small. I explain that I contacted Orlando to stay there for the next few days. He is quiet, and just nods. He seems suspicious of my story. He wasn't made aware of my arrival. He looks at my motorcycle, then back at me in full gear with helmet in hand.

"Well ziss is too facked up zoo be made up," he says with a shrug. He swings his arm, welcoming me into the house with his robe flapping open and shut.

Orlando is studying in San Jose and has three roommates who are college students as well. One is out of town and I am taking his room. His belongings are thrown around the room and I feel invasive as I arrange them to make room for my bags. There's a shattered bureau mirror and I notice splinters of glass, fresh on the ground. Signs of a short temper perhaps. I stop touching his things and awkwardly stack my bags into a tower in the corner.

The guys around the house are preoccupied with classes and personal engagements. To me, hospitality is like a waitress, there's a balance. I don't like my coffee going cold from neglect, but a scalding hot cup from obsessive attention isn't nice either. Orlando gives me the wifi password and shows me where the toilet is, a perfect balance.

Despite cool temperatures, Orlando is always shirtless, and Frenchy stopped putting on airs for me. He doesn't bother wearing a robe anymore. Orlando drinks water out of a vodka bottle from morning to evening.

"Zis man iz crahzay! He iz alwayz drinking!" Frenchy would joke.

The next day I check out the center square and parking is hard to find. I spot a McDonalds with a motorcycle parked in the entrance and there's room for one more. I sit perpendicular to traffic, blocking a lane of angry drivers beeping at me. I'm waiting for a gap to form in the endless sea of people crowding the sidewalk. My chance comes and I hop the high curb. Jenny's tires skid into the McDonald's corridor next to the other bike. All the customers are staring as I remove my big red suit, then a security guard tells me I can't park there. I point to the other motorcycle and ask why not. I am not a bother am I? He talks with the manager and he makes the same ruling.

I leave without a fuss, but the stir I caused leaves me puzzled. I soon realize the level of civility I brought to that situation. Launching myself into a place of business to park wasn't incredibly tactful. Especially when I questioned the security guard's request to move. I have become a little wilder and unruly. San Jose is not a bastion of etiquette, but I realize I have to tone things down a bit. Cultural osmosis is taking place and I feel a transfusion of fiery Latin blood coursing through my veins. This could just be another clever rationalization to justify my behavior. Maybe I'm just an inconsiderate ass.

This is the first time I have trouble finding a place to park so I opt for a bus from Orlando's. This is my first time on public transportation alone in Latin America. I'm not familiar with routes and who knows where it will take me. Besides, I like being in the driver's seat and in control of where I'm going despite not knowing where.

I walk around downtown while listening to the movie *My Dinner with Andre*. Listening to movies has been something I took up recently while riding. Quentin Tarantino movies are a favorite of mine for the brilliant dialog. I can imagine the movie as I am riding. In the case of *My Dinner with Andre*, it is only dialog. For two hours two men sit and talk over dinner. Andre was a theater director who has recently been traveling to strange places around the world. His dinner companion, Wallace, is a screenwriter who has worked with Andre long ago. Wallace is tied up with the day-to-day challenges of life, paying the bills, running errands, and looking for work. On the opposite extreme is Andre, a globetrotting free spirit unconcerned with the contingencies of life. I see myself turning into Andre, and I tell all my friends at home to watch or listen to the movie.

"You'll understand what I'm doing. Just watch it, it's brilliant!" I say.

Few of my friends make it through the full two hours. Of those that did, even fewer don't have a better understanding of what I am doing out here.

It's a valid question: what am I doing? I can't articulate it, but I can recognize some essence of my drive to travel in this movie. It has something to do with being, or a state of existence that is more vibrant than any other I have experienced before. I pause on a street corner to listen to one of the good parts:

---

WALLY: Right, because they just didn't see anything somehow, except the few little things that they wanted to see.

---

ANDRE: Yeah. You know, it's like what happened just before my mother died. You know, we'd gone to the hospital to see my mother, and I went in to see her. And I saw this woman who looked as bad as any survivor of Auschwitz or Dachau. And I was out in the hall, sort of comforting my father, when a doctor who is a specialist in a problem that she had with her arm, went into her room and came out just beaming. And he said: "Boy! Don't we have a lot of reason to feel great! Isn't it wonderful how she's coming along!" Now, all he saw was the arm, that's all he saw. Now, here's another person who's existing in a dream. Who on top of that is a kind of butcher, who's committing a kind of familial murder, because when he comes out of that room he psychically kills us by taking us into a dream world, where we become confused and frightened. Because the moment before we saw somebody who already looked dead and now here comes a specialist who tells us they're in wonderful shape! I mean, you know, they were literally driving my father crazy. I mean, you know, here's an eighty-two-year-old man who's very emotional, and, you know, if you go in one moment, and you see the person's dying, and you don't want them to die, and then a doctor comes out five minutes later and tells you they're in wonderful shape! I mean, you know, you can go crazy!

WALLY: Yeah, I know what you mean.

ANDRE: I mean, the doctor didn't see my mother. People at the public theater didn't see me. I mean, we're just walking around in some kind of fog. I think we're all in a trance! We're walking around like zombies! I don't think we're even aware of ourselves or our own reaction to things, we're just going around all day like unconscious machines, I mean, while there's all of this rage and

I've broken my trance now that I've put distance between myself and my former life, but I worry about slipping back into one when I return home, and think of techniques to keep this awareness alive.

It is Saturday night and I return to Orlando's house to make dinner in the kitchen. Rice and beans with some seasoning is my staple. Bags of pasta and bland tomato sauce are the household's staple. I see them eat the same thing every evening. Typical college kids. The guys have no classes and it is the first opportunity for us to hang out. Orlando offers me a swig of his water from his vodka bottle and I decline and hold up the water bottle I am never without. Frenchy is in the kitchen and cooking up something other than pasta this time. He's rubbing his nose and I noticed the lines of cocaine on the table.

"Would zoo like one?" he asked.

"Nah I'm good."

Orlando walks up to take his turn, and I smell a trail of cheap vodka. I realize it hadn't been water at all! My naivety had led me to believe he was just staying hydrated. He was constantly drinking and never looked drunk. I couldn't believe that someone could consume so much and still function at such a high level.

They invite me to join them at a club they are going to, but the guys party too hard for me. I have to leave early tomorrow and use it as my excuse to politely decline. Orlando asks me to wake him up in the morning and then they leave.

I am up at seven o'clock to get a jump on the day to try and make it to Panama. Orlando's door is open but his room is completely dark so I can't see a thing.

"Orlando, wake up!" I shout.

No answer. I can't find a light switch so I creep into the black and shake his bed. Still nothing. I don't know how this alcoholic coke-head is going to respond if I shake his leg, maybe with a groan or maybe with a fist. I get my flashlight and find he isn't even there and Frenchy isn't back either. What happened to them last night? It was something really good or really bad. Moderation is not a virtue these two possess. I leave a note with my thanks, and I ride off towards Panama, the next country and gateway to a new continent.

# DAY 112
# PANAMA CITY, PANAMA

"A friend is someone who knows all about you and still loves you."

Albert Hubbard

Latitude:    008° 59' 39" N
Longitude: 079° 31' 07" W

10,159 miles to Ushuaia

I'm waiting behind a wall that blocks the view of the security exit at the Panama City airport. Amber's flight just landed and she will be here any minute. Every time I pick her up at the airport, I sneak up behind her to scare her.

"What's in the bag miss?" I'd say in my best security guard voice, or "Hey blondie, where you going?" I'd whisper in my creepy voice.

I'm the only gringo around, with a big red beard, so it might be harder to pull this off here. She exits and her eyes dart around the room until they land on me. She runs up and presses her lips to mine, throwing her arms around me, grinding our teeth together with the force of the embrace. There are 100 people waiting for their loved ones, but they're all watching us now.

"Woo hoo!" goes someone in the background.

It's unreal to see her. She's here, in Panama. It feels like no time has passed, and nothing has changed. Amber hops on Jenny, and I take her into the controlled chaos of the city streets. We are heading back to the hostel where we are staying for the next few days. I am splitting through lanes of traffic and I feel Amber's fingers clenching around my waist. This is all new to her, and culture shock has a way of heightening when you're on the back of a motorcycle. I take it easy. There's no rush, I've got Jenny and Amber, my two girls.

We tour the city and take in the sights of a historical district. I'm stopped by a soldier as I try and turn around on a street that leads to the house of Panama's president. I resist the soldier's command until Amber translates for me. She doesn't know any Spanish but can listen and use her intuition to understand a situation better than I.

In the evening we mingle with other travelers in the common area of the hostel. I find the owner of a motorcycle parked next to mine with plates from El Salvador. It's a rickety 250cc, a smaller version of Jenny. He's a Frenchman who spent the last six months in Central America. He's returning home to his mother. She knows about his travels, but he left out the motorcycle part so he's selling it before he returns home. Roger is an American checking out homes to retire. The coast is littered with high rises like Miami but the majority of them are condos, catering to the growing number of people like Roger. Panama uses the US Dollar as their currency which makes the transition easier. Amber is getting tired of the city and wants to explore more of the country. Panama City is similar to most cities in the US and it's a reason why we are meeting a lot of Americans. I want to show her something different, a taste of what I have been experiencing.

We head to Bocas del Toro, a full day ride to the northwest corner of Panama. There is an island, Isla Colon, where there are good beaches. It starts raining hard, and we stop a hundred miles shy in Gualaca, a small mountain town. Amber is transferred to another era, with dirt roads and men on horseback. I have adjusted to these things, and watching her take it all in is like experiencing it for the first time again. There's a chicken coop in the backyard of the hotel we're staying at. We watch the chickens being chickens, and anthropomorphize their behavior. There's a loud thunder crack in the distance, then the power goes out.

The next morning we arrive at the dock where a transport ferry will take us to the island, but we just missed its daily voyage, so we spend the evening on the mainland. At dinner we are approached by the restaurant owner. Woody is curious about our story and we share where we're from and where we're going.

"Ah the US, it's been a decade since I lived there," he says.

"Oh yea? Where?"

"A few places. I couldn't stay long. I wanted to have a big family and I couldn't do that in the US."

"Why not?"

"It's too damn expensive! You've got daycare, school, and doctor visits. After raising two kids in the US I moved back to Panama to raise six more for less money than the first two."

"How do you manage that?"

"You have to do everything on your own in the US, or pay someone to help out. Here in Panama the community helps. You don't pay someone to watch your child. You ask a neighbor, and help them when they ask you in turn."

"I never really thought about that."

"I love the US, but I just can't afford it. Besides, Panama is my true home."

Our food arrives and Amber and I have a rousing discussion involving American values. We head to bed early and are woken by a racket outside. It's a Christmas parade with three floats and the whole town is in the streets. It takes five minutes to pass and we get the sense of community Woody was talking about.

The next day, we hop the ferry and arrive on the island in the afternoon. We immediately start looking for a place to stay. I can't afford most and the others are booked. I didn't plan anything and typically things fall into place on their own. Amber is a planner and this whole approach drives her crazy.

"We'll find something," I assure her.

A room is open at the end of the island with everything we need. We drop our bags and explore the beaches via water taxis. Amber snorkels for the first time and falls in love with it.

"Every vacation from this point needs to include snorkeling," she declares.

There's a road that runs out of town and we hop on Jenny to check it out. The island stretches for ten miles and it's not long before we are on the other side. Biology students frequent the island to study the wildlife and soon we notice rustling in the tree tops from monkeys, and a herd of Amber's favorite animal crowds the road.

"Goats! I love goats!" I hear her scream through her helmet. She slaps my sides with excitement. We reach the end of the island and the track turns to deep soft sand. I paddle my way through until Jenny's back wheel sinks and we wobble over at a slow speed. I flop over and Amber has rolled off.

"Are you OK?!" I ask.
"That was fun!" she shouts as her muffled laughs emerge from her helmet.

We make another attempt through the sand.

"I think you need to go faster!" she says.
"Yes dear," I shoot back at her as I struggle through the sand.

A back seat rider is hard to ignore when they are hugging your waist and shouting in your ear.

---

"Attention Nerds", a sign reads back at the hostel. Further down it says, "Free beer for technical support. Ask for Dan." I ask for Dan and he's got a laptop with a screen that keeps turning on and off while he uses it for performances.

"I'm not really a hardware guy, but I can give it a shot." I say sheepishly.

"I need to get a new laptop if this doesn't get fixed, so even if you know a little that'd be awesome if you can check it out."

Three hours later Dan has a functional screen with a broken track pad.

"Sorry about the track pad. You can easily get an external mouse, but at least your screen works now."

"Yes! Thank you so much!" Dan screams and follows with a bear hug. Amber and I drink free for the rest of the afternoon and evening.

The next morning we sleep in, but are woken up by the sound of a loud motor roaming the grounds of the hostel. I am taken back in time to my apartment complex in Phoenix where weed whackers and leaf blowers used to wake me up.

"It's just some landscaping guys. Go back to bed sweetie."

"Are you sure?" she asks.

"Yes, I am sure. Go back to bed."

I'm not sure, but I really want to go back to sleep.

"Bill!" Amber screams.

"It's just a weed whacker! God knows why they give a shit about the landscape around this dump."

"Bill! There's smoke!" Amber points.

"God damn it!"

Smoke is pouring through the gap beneath our door. There's obviously a fire, but we're thinking two different things at the same time.

"Why does this fire have to ruin my life?" thinks Amber.

"Why does this fire have to ruin my sleep?" I think.

I storm out of the door in my underwear and find two guys donning gas masks in protective suits spraying smoke everywhere with noisy motors on their back. Amber and I put clothes on and head to the curb with the rest of the guests and staff. I walk up to a girl who works at the hostel.

"Dude!" I say and startle her.
"Umm what?" she asks, surprised.
"What the fuck is happening?"
"They are spraying for bed bugs."
"No one let us know it was happening. We got woken up by that shit."
"Aw really? I am so sorry!" she says with her dopey face.

Normally I would demand to speak to her supervisor, but there's two problems: 1) there isn't a supervisor in this joint, and 2) I'm hungry. I cover my mouth and reenter to grab my wallet and take Amber out to breakfast. We walk down the main strip and I do a double take as we pass a motorcycle.

"Look at this honey, an African Twin!"
"Yea it's great," Amber humors me.
"It even has a scrolling map holder. I wonder if this guy races off road!"
"Hum, yea maybe. Can we get breakfast now?"
"This is no local. He's gotta be traveling around like me."
"Yea maybe, c'mon. Let's go!"
"Hey look! Guatemala plates! I've never seen a bike like this with Central American plates."

Amber points out the drool on my face and we continue on our way. I can smell my own kind very well, and all my inhibitions are dropped when I see another motorcycle traveler. Too bad I didn't get to run into him.

We board the boat heading back to the mainland. As I roll Jenny down the steel deck I notice the African Twin parked at the end. A man is leaning against the railing, looking out over the water.

"Nice bike," I say.

"Thanks," he answers.

This is the best way to open a conversation with a fellow motorcyclist. His name is Indy and he's been riding around Central America for a few months. He's a watercraft mechanic back in Canada. He works six months a year and takes the rest of his free time to travel.

"I'm running out of places to go," he says.

He travels alone with a small bag and a guitar. I envy his minimalism and it makes me wonder if I really need all the things I take with me. We swap stories for the duration of the boat ride and take off together on the only road out of town. Amber and I watch Indy while he stays within eyesight. Strapped to his back, his guitar is the last thing we see after he picks up speed and disappears over a hill.

---

For Christmas Day we stop at a beach on the Pacific coast. We cut off the main road to Playa las Lajas and are met with a military checkpoint ten miles before the coast. It's a routine documentation check, but five miles later there is another checkpoint. They check our papers again and ask if we have any glass bottles. Hundreds of broken bottles lay on the side of the road. They are serious about the no glass rule.

We arrive at the beach to find it half deserted, but there is a strong military presence. Trucks patrol the beach and officers walk up and down it in pairs. The heavy military presence doesn't seem justified on such a peaceful beach, but we don't pay much attention to it.

"More the merrier," we think.

We set up camp under a cabana near the water. A couple of workers are chopping fresh bamboo and constructing more cabanas nearby. With massive forearms and leathery palms they hack away with their machetes with a precision entertaining enough to sit and watch.

The beach is peppered with hundreds of figures in the sand that resemble a bursting firework frozen in time. A large hole stands at the center while concentric circles made up of small balls of sand circle it. The explanation for this phenomenon pops out of the holes behind us after we are a few paces away. Crabs are sifting through the sand for nutrients and leaving small balls of sand behind. Their survival depends on scurrying back to their home in the sand. I sprint forward to provoke their retreat, each crab blazing a trail to its own hole. How they know which one is theirs, who knows? I catch one off guard, and in a panic it runs into a hole that is already occupied. The crab is forced out by the other and it repeats this process in surrounding locations until it finally makes its way back to its own hole.

"Leave the poor guys alone!" Amber scolds at me.

I justify my behavior with notions of Darwinian survival amid a world growing too soft.

"Maybe you're an ass who happens to have a vocabulary to justify whatever you please," she shoots back.

When she's right, she's right.

With a fresh seafood dinner and 75 cent beers, we slowly become disillusioned with the tradition of eggnog around the fireplace and a white Christmas. We watch the sunset over the ocean then head to bed. This is how to celebrate the holidays.

It is one o'clock in the morning and we wake up to a man

mumbling nearby. I think he is walking around and talking on his cellphone. This continues for a while and finally I pop my head out of the tent. The man is sitting a couple feet away on our bench, with a bottle in his hand, drunk as hell. I ask him what he wants, but I can't understand his slurring and stammering. I stand up and shine my flashlight to find one of the cabana workers. I had been watching them swing their machetes with a surgical precision earlier. I don't see the machete on him, but it's common for locals to walk around with them. The wind died down and the tent is swelteringly hot. Amber is having a claustrophobic panic attack during all this.

"Bill, I need to get out of this tent, now!" she insists.

"Not now honey!"

I have no idea what is going on with this drunk, potentially machete wielding man, four feet away. She sticks her head out of the tent and I shine my flashlight on the man again.

"We're trying to sleep, please go away," I ask politely.

He doesn't budge. I try every polite way to ask the him to leave, but still nothing. Over ten minutes my patience diminishes as my voice rises and eventually Spanish is pouring out of me effortlessly.

"Go away! Why are you bothering us? I don't want any trouble." I shout and take closer steps towards him.

My heart is pounding. He leaves and I breathe a sigh of relief.

"Where the hell are the patrols when you need them?!" I ask no one as Amber recovers from her claustrophobia.

There are no more creatures stirring until four o'clock when we wake up to hundreds of ants climbing over our feet. I left salami in the tent and the ants are devouring it. We sleep together in my hammock, which works for about an hour, until I wake up with a horrible pain in my back. I sleep on a bench until sunrise.

Amber wakes up as I pack up camp. I lift up the tent and a huge crab scurries away.

"I knew it! You son of a bitch!" Amber screams.

"What the hell are you talking about?" I ask.

Amber goes on to tell me how she had been woken up throughout the night by a scratching noise near her ear which turned out to be the place where this crab decided to dig his new home. We both started a sleep deprived hysterical laugh as we recount all the events of the past six hours. A drunken machete wielding cabana worker, an infestation of ants and a crab who knows nothing of personal boundaries. Far from a Christmas Eve without creatures stirring, but a night we'll never forget.

# DAY 130
# THE CARIBBEAN SEA

"Without a doubt, there is something satisfying about being immersed in nature, about relying on long-forgotten skills dusty from disuse, and about stripping away many of the distractions that clutter our lives. Nature has the power to change our perspective, to make us reassess what is important."

Rowboat in a Hurricane by Julie Angus

Latitude:   010° 08' 30" N
Longitude: 077° 00' 34" W

9,195 miles to Ushuaia

After two weeks Amber has to return home and now I'm catching a boat to Columbia, a missing link in the Pan-American Highway. The obstacle is called the Darien Gap and it stretches for 100 miles through southern Panama and Northern Columbia. It consists of thick forests and mangroves. The first vehicular crossing took 136 days with a team of people fighting through the swamps. I never like taking a detour due to difficult terrain, but this is an obstacle worthy of an exception.

I have been fantasizing about crossing the sea for weeks. I've never been on a boat for more than a couple hours and the idea of spending six days on the open water peaks my interest. I think the ocean has similar characteristics to the deserts I love so much. The vast emptiness and geographic solitude puts me in a state of peace. I won't be dodging potholes and feel it will give me time to reflect on the new continent that awaits me.

I ride two hours north of Panama City to Portobelo. Idling through the streets of the small town I notice a horrible mud slide spanning 100 feet. Houses are ripped apart with kitchens and bedrooms exposed to the open air. Decorations are intact on the walls, and I feel like I am intruding on privacy they no longer have.

The harbor is not much more inviting with the sight of a sunken ship, with its mast sticking out of the water at a 45 degree angle. I try and read the partially submerged flag to see if it's the ship I am supposed to board, but I spot mine, Fritz the Cat, and the captain waves in acknowledgement of my presence. I'm two hours early and wait on the edge of the dock. It's the end of the road for Jenny. She will be sunbathing for the next week on top of the deck.

Other passengers start trickling into town and I'm delighted to see that there are four other riders like myself. Simon from Canada on a BMW F800GS, Marcus from Germany on a BMW F1200GS and an Aussie couple, Chris and Allen, on a KLR 250 and KLR 650 respectively. Simon is heading for Ushuaia like myself and Marcus wants to travel through Peru without much of an itinerary beyond that. Chris and Allen started in Seattle, Washington and are going every which way they can. They thought they would be home by now, but eight months later here they are a third the distance they anticipated. I envy their pace. The rest are here for the experience of a gourmet chef (also the captain) and stops at the clear waters of the San Blas islands off the coast of Panama.

There never seems to be any shortage of Aussies no matter where I go. Marika and Damien are another Aussie couple on board. Oliver and Philip are backpackers from the Netherlands. Sierra is from South Africa and studies in Costa Rica with Jennifer, who is American as far as I'm concerned, but identifies herself as French. Then there's Bjorn from Switzerland who is traveling on his own like me. The captain, Fritz, is German along with his wife whose name I can never remember. The ship's capacity is 16 and we are 14 altogether.

The motorcycles are to be strapped down on the deck of the catamaran, a two hulled ship with a central cockpit. I wonder how we are going to get the bikes on board, especially Marcus's huge 1200GS. Fritz starts securing a narrow board for a ramp. We start with Simon's F800GS. It's heavier than Jenny so if that can make it, she should be able to as well. Bjorn worked on boats before and he's at Fritz's side like a hired deckhand. Fritz barks orders in a thick German accent and everyone shuffles around the bike accordingly. Three are pushing at the back and two are pulling from the front. There's wobbling and grunting but eventually we roll her onboard. Chris and Marcus' bikes go up without a problem.

It's Jenny's turn, and I hop on her to steer while people push and pull. Her front wheel rolls onto the ramp as the wind picks up. The boat is drifting and the ramp is sliding all over the deck. The gap between the hull and the dock is growing and I feel like Jenny is going to fall in the water. Fritz aborts the attempt until the winds calm down. We tighten the ropes that hold the ship in place against the dock and make another attempt. My heart is in my throat, but before I know it I am on the deck of the ship and slapping the backs of everyone who helped. It's Allen's turn with his KLR650. He lines up with the ramp and waves away people coming to help. With a cigarette hanging from his lip, right eye squinting shut from the smoke, he guns it and rides up the ramp like it were a speed bump. I love Aussies.

The bikes are secured on the deck and everyone is strapping garbage bags onto their bikes to protect from the salt water. I forgot about this precaution and don't bother.

"A little salt water won't hurt Jenny, she's bulletproof." I think to myself.

We get settled into our quarters. I'm in the common living area in a claustrophobic crevice, having to step over Marcus, Simon and Bjorn to get in and out of bed. Luckily tight spaces don't bother me, and I prefer them. Two hatch doors open above my head to bring in a breeze from the open water. The main communal area is at the rear of the ship. There's at least ten people there at any given time. I haven't been in a group social setting in months and all the overlapping voices are raising my anxiety levels.

"Six days of this," I think to myself.

It's been four months of solitary travel and I had gotten used to it, so this is a shock to my system. I handled the madness of Honduras better. I take a break at the bow of the ship and chase an extra dose of anti-anxiety medication with a beer.

We stay in the harbor for the first evening and leave in the morning. I am having trouble sleeping. It's not my fellow passengers that keep me up. I'm picturing the whole of South America and the distance I need to travel. I've been on the road for four months and 10,000 miles. I have to cover another 10,000 and the road conditions get worse the farther south. I do the math: 10,000 miles over four months is about 100 miles per day. Not a grueling pace at all. I try and trust the math.

The milestone of a new continent is stirring anxiety in me that I hadn't anticipated. I am used to Central America, and now I'm leaving it for a new land. It's like crossing into Mexico all over again, but this time I can't turn around and ride back to the US. It never was a thought that I had, nor is it easy if I wanted to return home while I was all the way down in Panama. I am breaking away from North America without an option for returning home by land and it makes me feel more isolated.

We arrive at the islands and it's time to snorkel. Bjorn is diving into the water with a harpoon, looking for lobsters. The current is strong and without fins I wouldn't be able to break away from it. Simon isn't a great swimmer and it's not long before he is back on the boat. I swim around an island that breaks the current so I can float in calm waters while fish, whose names I'll never know, dance around me.

Back on the boat, the group dynamic is irritating. When someone is talking, most are waiting for their turn to talk. Some with bigger egos interrupt with an anecdote to best the other. I give up on talking in the group's presence and wait to converse with individuals when I can. Someone compliments Sierra's tattoo on her wrist. It's a bunch of stars of varying sizes with a loose grouping. I noticed it days ago.

"Is there some significance to it?" I ask.

"I was in a coffee shop with my sister. We had learned that there was a tattoo parlor above it and I decided to go and get a tattoo. I picked out something I liked and that was that." she says.

"Hmm, just like that eh?"

"Yea...", her head tilted up in reflection, "...it represents a very special moment between my sister and I."

Jennifer interrupts with an anecdote she read in "The Ascent of Money: A Financial History of the World". She makes it apparent to everyone she was reading something interesting, but none of us give a shit.

"That's great Jennifer," I say.

My head turns back towards Sierra.

"I always ask people about the meaning behind their tattoo. I am always curious. I've never heard of anyone getting a tattoo to represent a moment. I like that. I spent years meticulously planning a tattoo I wanted to get, but I never went through with it. I could never think of a concept, an idea, or a sentiment that didn't have the potential of being wrong later on in my life. A moment though, well I think that's beautiful."

I am a recovering philosophy major. The decay of my inordinate intellectualism I approached life with had been accelerating since I started my journey. I picture myself laying on my belly getting "TDF" tattoo on my back when I reach Ushuaia. It stands for "Tierra Del Fuego", the state of Ushuaia, representing this whole journey and hundreds of moments.

We spend New Years Eve with our anchor down near some islands. There are celebrations happening on an island and we get permission from Fritz to ring in the new year on land.

We are taken to the island on a small dingey. Our first sight is a goat being cooked over fiery coals like a lean-to tent. The party is already in swing and everyone is inviting and warm. The island is inhabited by the Kuna people of Panama. A generator runs a fridge keeping the two dollar beers cold and fueling the 100+ party throughout the evening.

After several failed attempts to start a fire, I steal hot coals from a nearby fire that has been abandoned. I carry the scalding shovel to our kindling, leaving a fiery bread crumb trail. I and the men in our group lost "man points" for failing to start a fire.

I've developed a crush over Sierra and I strategically position myself next to her as we circle the fire. I change the music Simon put on to mine. His playlist of "cock rock" wasn't the best and once AC/DC came on it was the last straw so I put on something more mellow.

"This is too sad," says Simon.

"Are you sad?" I ask.

He says nothing.

"I like it," Sierra says.

I smile and go on to explain the band's discography in way too much detail. Everyone is having a good time around the fire and no one on the island has noticed that midnight has passed and it's 12:07 A.M. I stand up and pretend it's a minute before midnight.

"It's 11:59 P.M. everybody! One minute to the new year!"

Everybody jumps to their feet.

"Thirty Seconds!

Everyone in earshot is gathering around our fire as I count down.

"Fifteen seconds!"

My eyes dart to Sierra. She's walking to Jennifer. I wasn't planning on kissing her at midnight, but as she moves away my heart drops. I feign excitement.

"Ten seconds!"

Half the island is surrounding me, lovers pair up, and I remember how much I hate being alone on new years. I switch the countdown to Spanish.

"Cinco!"

This is usually when I walk out of the party.

"Cuatro!"

Watching others embrace makes it worse.

"Tres!"

I stop looking at the imaginary countdown on my watch.

"Dos!"

Everyone else is carrying the count and my voice is no longer necessary.

"Uno!" everyone shouts in unison.

I start wandering away from the group.

"Feliz nuevo años!" the island exclaims.

I head for the shore but I'm intercepted with hugs from my shipmates and whatever stranger who happens to make eye contact with me. A depressing evening is turned around in a minute and for the first time as a single man, I enjoy myself.

The next morning we hit the open sea for Cartagena. It will take three days and this has been the part I've been anticipating the most, open water with nothing in sight. I take a seat at the bow and sit watching the water rush by. The ship crawls up large swells and tips down. I am getting soaked and thrown around. I try out my impression of Lieutenant Dan from the movie Forest Gump.

"Arrr the seas are angry!" laughing like a madman.

I head back to the cockpit for more coffee to find everyone half asleep. Sierra is the only one active and I ask what's going on. She tells me that sleepiness is a mild form of sea sickness. Like rocking a baby to sleep. I head back to the bow.

The waves are getting more intense and my arms get tired from holding my butt in place. I rig up a harness with some parachute cord so I can lean back, and now I have my very own recliner at the best seat in the house.

Flying fish dart out of the water and skip across it. I hear splashing of a sort I hadn't heard before. I look below my dangling feet and gasp with excitement. I scream towards the back of the ship:

"Dolphins!"

There's a dozen of them and they are jumping out of the water in front of the ship. One guy isn't jumping. He swims right under me and turns to the side to look up at me. The others are jumping in twos and threes in perfect sequence. After ten minutes they get bored and recede back into the water.

Jennifer and I are both reading while everyone else is passed out or too nauseous to speak.

"What are you reading?" she asks.
"It's called, Rowboat in a Hurricane. It's about a woman and a man rowing across the Atlantic ocean."

"Why on Earth would you read that at a time like this?" she recoils.

"I like reading about adventures."

I've never been on a boat, and I wasn't sure how I would react to it. No matter how bad it gets here, I know it was worse for them. As I read on I envy them though. I share a passage with her.

---

"This row across the Atlantic Ocean will create memories that you will take to your grave. The dolphins, the sharks, the storms, the struggles-it's all priceless. Your years of work will all blur into one another. But this year won't. Believe me, forty years down the road, you're not going to kick yourself for having rowed across an ocean."

---

"It reminds me of what I am doing, but they are relying on their muscles to bring them across the ocean. How amazing is that?!"

"It sounds horrible," she says before going back to her book.

After dinner I notice a sticker of Fiona, from the movie Shrek, on Marcus's motorcycle luggage. I ask him about it and it turns out that's what he named his bike.

"She is ugly, and strong, but she has a big heart." he explains.

I tell him how I have trouble naming my bike. First it was Hermes, the Greek god of travel, but that didn't stick. Next it was Phobos, an irregularly shaped moon of Mars. My bike is ugly, irregularly shaped, and I like the sound of it, but it doesn't have a feminine touch that I always regard her with. Also, I don't care for riding boys.

Marcus leaps to his feet and announces a challenge for everyone. A beer goes to the person who comes up with a name for my bike and everyone starts shouting suggestions all at once.

"Sophie!"

"Tina!"

"Roberta!"

Nothing strikes me.

After everyone quiets down, Sierra chimes up and asks,

"What's your favorite movie?"

"Forest Gump" I answer.

"What was the name of that girl?"

Everyone shouts, "Jenny!" and then start to do their best Forest impressions.

"Jen-aye!"

"Jen-nee!"

"Jan-nay!"

A smile comes to my face and I'm sold. It's perfect. All my subsequent motorcycles can be named in sequence: Jenny II, Jenny III and so on. Just like the fleet of shrimping boats that made up Bubba Gump Shrimp Company. It fits an important criteria I have for dog names: don't exceed two syllables. Anything more than that and it makes it harder to shout when they are being bad. I can picture myself broken down in the middle of the Andes, shouting, "come on Jenny!" Later that evening Sierra writes "Jenny" on my gas tank and it becomes official.

We are halfway to Cartagena in the middle of the sea. I know this because of my GPS. We are going 2.5 MPH and have 100 miles more to cover. Forty more hours. I ask Fritz and my estimates are close. I'm wide awake, but force my eyes shut to try and sleep.

Around one o'clock in the morning I wake up to a lot of noise from the cockpit. Damien storms into the kitchen to grab a large bowl. Fritz and his wife are shouting back and forth to each other and Marcus has a worried expression. I jump to the conclusion that the ship is sinking and the bowl is for bailing. How could a ship of this sophistication not have a bilge pump? That makes no sense. I get up to settle the argument I'm having with myself.

The bowl is for Marika who is puking from the rough seas. The rule is to puke off the back of the ship, but this is not an option because a support beam has broken loose from the corner of the roof that covers the cabin. There is no longer a lifeline to hold onto and anyone can go overboard easily. You have a 20% chance of being found again. The motor for the autopilot has an oil leak and a buzzer is indicating it's running low. Marcus and Fritz's wife are trying to fill a canister with oil. They are spilling it everywhere because they couldn't find the funnel.

Fritz breaks his German and shouts, "Oh for fucks sake!" and starts rummaging through a compartment to find the funnel.

I take the captain's chair and man the wheel while he does the repairs. "Don't worry everyone, I've got her" I think as I correct our bearing on 75 degrees east. I don't think anyone can keep their ego from growing when they sit in something called the "Captains chair", especially not me.

"Marcus! You call that deck clean?! Mop up that spilled oil!"

"Damien! Secure a new life line across the stern!"

"Fritz's wife! It's been four days and it has passed the socially acceptable time to ask your name, but now I'm the captain! What the hell is your name?!"

Fritz claims his seat back and my internal power trip is over. It felt good even for an imaginary one.

The autopilot is restored, the beam is secure and Marika stops puking. Everyone returns to sleep and I am delegated on watch for the next two hours. Fritz's orders are to watch the temperature gauge for overheating, listen for any buzzers that go off, make sure the needle is on 75 degrees East and look for running lights of ships we may crash into. I am to wake him up if any of that goes wrong.

The winds are not in our favor and we are propelled by motor. The whirring of the engines are hypnotic. Five minutes ago everything was crazy, and now it's just me and the inky black sea.

I went on a road trip years ago with four friends of mine. We all piled into a SUV and headed across the US for 5,000 miles over nine days. When I took my turn to drive, the fact that I was responsible for my friends lives always flew into the forefront of my mind. Just a quick swerve a few degrees and they're all dead. Their death felt more material than my own.

I'm alone in the cockpit and I feel responsible for 16 lives. I check the gauges compulsively and wonder if Fritz's decision to put me on watch was wise. I talk some sense to myself:

"Stop being so melodramatic you schmuck. You're looking at a couple dials and watching for lights out on the water. You're not delivering organs."

The waves and winds are getting stronger. I feel the ship slowly crawl up the waves and quickly slip back down. It's like a roller coaster in slow motion. A huge wave crashes over the bow and a flying fish washes onto the deck. I can't just leave him there, but I squirm at the idea of touching a fish. He's only 6 inches long, but his flippers are longer than he is. I make a quick stab at him with my hand and it feels like putting my hand into a rubber fan, but I manage to chuck him back in the water.

I should have given my watch over to Marcus an hour ago, but I'm still wide awake. This is the first moment I feel alone in the middle of the sea. Riding solo for four months isn't enough. I have to be at the helm of a ship plunging through the water, hundreds of miles from land. I fantasize getting to the Salar de Uyuni. It is a salt flat that is 25 times the size of the Bonneville Salt Flats in Nevada. It's a sea of white nothingness. When it rains, it leaves a never ending mirror stretching to the horizon that you can't discern because it reflects the sky. I fantasize about camping here for a couple days. I want to do it blind. I am going to put a blindfold over my eyes, and feel what it's like to experience the world without sight. The Salar de Uyuni seems fitting because I can't trip over much. I have thousands of feet of fishing line just for this. One end will be tied to Jenny, and the other to me. I can walk wherever I want and find my way back to camp. It's my fifth hour at watch and I finally turn over my duties to Marcus for some much needed sleep.

The next day, I attach a safety line to my electronic reader as I sit on the bow and read. A few strong waves knock me out of my harness. My hands reach for the rails and my reader falls to my side dangling from it's digital life line. I start to see the virtue of cheap paperbacks. Everyone is sick of the sea and sleeping for most of the day. I think this is something I could get used to. After sunset we see lights and slip into Cartagena's harbor. Everyone is dead silent and awestruck by the sight of land. I go inside to pack my belongings, eager to get back on Jenny.

# DAY 135
# CARTAGENA, COLOMBIA

"Go confidently in the direction of your dreams.
Live the life you've imagined."

Henry David Thoreau

Latitude:    010° 23' 14" N
Longitude: 075° 31' 10" W

8,785 miles to Ushuaia

---

I hear a siren and outside I see a police boat docking with an officer boarding. He has a stern grimace and everyone is frozen except for Fritz. He is scrutinizing everything, and asks to see everyone's passport. Fritz greets the officer with a bag of the passports he collected from us and another bag full of beer. He cracks one open and Fritz does too. Everything checks out and he returns to his boat, tossing beers to the other officers on board.

I share a room with Simon and Marcus at a hotel to reduce costs. We're all cheap, but I'm the cheapest. There's a single and a double bed. Marcus opts to pay more of the room's share for a guaranteed spot in a bed. Which bed he gets is up to Simon and me, but Simon mostly. If Simon and I share a bed neither of us has to sleep on the floor. I propose a head to toe configuration and Simon isn't saying anything. I offer to sleep on top of the covers in my sleeping bag. He offers to pay more for the room and suddenly my share is only ten bucks. I sleep well on my sleeping pad on the floor.

I do all I care to do as a tourist on the first day in Cartagena and spend the next day sitting in cafes. Our passports have been processed through Fritz. As the captain, he is held accountable for all parties entering the country. There is a delay and we will have our passports tomorrow.

"He can't do this!" Jennifer bursts.

"He just did," says Simon, and I laugh inside.

Jennifer pouts and tells Sierra she'll call her father to sort things out. I wonder what her Daddy can do to fix this inconvenience. I picture his monocle falling to the ground after his cheek muscles react in shock over the treatment of his little princess.

The next day we get our passports and motorcycles off the boat. Simon is in a hurry to get his bike to the immigration office and get going. Fritz gives Marcus a piece of paper with directions to the immigration office. Allen and Chris are busy with a hacksaw on a luggage padlock seized with corrosion due to the salt water. Simon is getting impatient, grabs the directions from Marcus and hops on his bike. There's some argument between them. Simon shoves the piece of paper in Marcus' chest, then rides away. I am getting sick of him anyways.

For our last night in Cartagena the whole group gets together for dinner. It has only been a week, but I have gotten close to everyone in my own little way. I will miss most of them.

I have a huge continent ahead of me to cross and I have more miles to cover in less time than it took for me to reach this point. The days will be longer, and the miles will be harder. I want to blast through the back roads of the Andes. The easy routes are boring, and I will feel like I hadn't been anywhere.

Doubt is running through my mind. I keep looking at maps of South America, and what I am trying to do seems impossible. I look at Central America, and my eyes retrace all the roads and memories. The only thing propelling me forward is looking back on the miles I have ridden. It seems unreal that I made it this far. I think back to the Mexico border. The same anxieties that consumed me then are creeping back up now.

"You're riding a motorcycle for a long time, you schmuck. You're not curing cancer. Quit being a pussy and just ride," I tell myself.

I wonder if I'll ever write a book about this whole thing. I picture the cover and everything. It's a picture of me looking at myself in a bathroom mirror, screaming at myself while crying. The title reads:

"Billy Berates Himself Across the Americas"

---

It takes an hour to exit Cartagena. I thought it might take two, so I'm ahead of schedule. One hundred miles later and Jenny is violently cutting in and out. She has enough fuel, I've never seen her act up like this. She stalls on the side of the road and after a couple minutes, starts back up. This happens a few more times, but she eventually starts back up again. There is a problem but I don't want there to be, so I ignore it and keep riding.

I'm climbing a steep hill and she dies for good this time. Across the street is a metal shop. An old woman sees me struggling and troubleshooting in the hot sun. She waves me over and offers me some shade to work in. She directs me to a motorcycle shop that I passed five miles ago. I write down her instructions and start pushing Jenny down the road.

Ten minutes later an oncoming motorcycle cop passes me, then turns around towards me. I'm pushing Jenny on the side of a busy street and I wonder if I'm going to get a ticket. He offers to give me a tow and I am worried how we can pull this off safely. I start pulling out rope, but he shakes his head and tells me to get on the bike. He positions his motorcycle behind my left shoulder and puts his boot firmly against my luggage rack. I realize he's going to push me with his motorcycle. He starts his bike and we're off.

I didn't have a chance to put on my helmet so the wind is blasting against my face and I realize how nice the wind feels against bare skin. We stay at a steady 10 MPH then increase to 15, then 20. He is talking into his radio but I can't make out what he's saying. Another motorcycle cop joins us and now he's behind my right shoulder. I feel a tug at my right luggage and both of them are pushing me. Their legs rest on the motorcycle crash bars with a hand on their hips. This is what I call a police escort!

With both of them pushing I reach 50 MPH. It feels weird going this fast without hearing Jenny's engine. The officer on my left points to the motorcycle shop and they pull ahead of me as I coast into the shop down a dirt path. I wave many thanks to them until they are out of sight. Jenny is broke, but my anxieties about Colombia have been washed away with this good deed. At the shop I'm the center of attention. Guys from the streets are walking up to check out Jenny and me.

"That motorcycle is really big, no?" a man asks.
"Yea, it's really heavy," I reply.

The mechanic is cranking Jenny over and listening intently to diagnose the problem. She starts up, but dies after a couple minutes. He starts ripping her apart and I look over his shoulder like a worried mother. This is why they don't let family in the operating room.

Something is gunked up from the sound Jenny is making. Methodically he cleans the air filter, battery terminals, and fuel hose. He starts Jenny after each component is cleaned to narrow down the problem. She's still clunking out when he revs her up high. He lets out a heavy sigh and starts gutting the carburetor. He cleans everything and reassembles everything. Still nothing. It's been three hours and more people have gathered. A boy notices the headlight flickering. The mechanic smirks and starts testing connections between wires with an electrical multimeter tool. He finds nothing.

It's been four hours and I'm starving. I get a late lunch next door.

When I return the mechanics is taking apart the components on my handlebars. I'm not sure why, but they keep at it. I start looking for hotel rooms. I don't think I'll make it out of here today. He starts Jenny again to see if she'll die again. She is screaming at 6,000 RPMs, there's no sign of her dying and everyone starts smiling. A faulty kill switch is the culprit.

This switch has three states: left Off, center On, and right Off. If I am stuck under Jenny and her wheels are still spinning, it's a very important switch to prevent further injury. The mechanic bypasses the kill switch and now I have to turn the key to kill the engine. Jenny is running great and we are free to eat up a hundred miles before we lose the light.

I decide not to camp in Colombia and stick to major roads. The kidnapping boogie man is in the back of my mind, and although I've come a long way to squash my paranoia, Colombia remains a place where I can't control it. The military presence on the road is outstanding, patrols are everywhere. Tourism is a major commodity for the country and they are taking huge steps to protect it.

I keep hearing a tip for tourists, it's even printed in my guide book. Supposedly it is not uncommon for FARC members (often associated with drug cartels) to impersonate military officials. If you come across an official, you are supposed to look at their boots. If they are leather, they are a legitimate official. If they are rubber, they are a FARC member. When you are standing at a distance where you can't identify the material of a man's boots, I'm not sure how this information is valuable.

Despite the horror stories, I feel safe in this country. I've gone through the growing pains of exposure to a foreign land while I was in Central America. Machete or gun wielding individuals don't phase me like they used to. It's simply a tool they use. Replace it with a laptop and you have an equivalent person in a developed nation going off to work.

I'm sixty miles north of the Ecuadorian border and slow down for a military checkpoint. I flash a thumbs up at them, expecting the same signal returned. The guy motions me to stop, but I keep going out of habit and I quickly turn around to go through the typical checkpoint dance I'm all too familiar with. The guard asks for my papers, glances over them, and turns his attention to me. He's asking me all kinds of questions and I realize he's just curious.

I take off my helmet and get more comfortable. It's hot and take off my boots too. He's really interested in Jenny. He sits on her pursing his lips approvingly. Then he asks if he can take her for a spin and before I realize what I'm doing I've tossed the keys to him. I watch him disappear over a hill with Jenny, my whole world.

He returns a few minutes later with a big smile. He likes Jenny. I start putting on my gear to hit the road, but he invites me to stay for lunch. I want to make it to the border before nightfall and tell him I don't have time. He insists and I agree. The border will be there tomorrow.

The other guards are sitting in the shade of a tent and I join them at a table. The guard orders a baby-faced soldier to pick up lunch. I see a standard issue military motorcycle and start talking shop with the rest of the guys. Motorcycles have a way of bringing people of any culture together. The soldier returns with a bag full of Chinese food boxes. There's only a dozen buildings that make up this desolate checkpoint in southern Colombia, and one of them happens to be a Chinese take-out shop. Sometimes things aren't so different.

We keep talking bikes and they ask if I wanted to take their motorcycle for a spin. I jump at the opportunity and throw my boots back on. I throw my leg over and hope Jenny isn't watching me with another. She's fast and the speed reminds me of my sport bike back home. I won't be stupid enough to run from a guy with one of these like I tried to in Nicaragua. As if running in the first place isn't a bad idea already. I return and we finish our lunch. We exchange gratitude for sharing time with each other, and I'm off to Ecuador. Too little time and too little known about such a wonderful country.

My fears did not come true. I did not get kidnaped by guerrilla FARC members, not even once. Maybe I was just lucky. I haven't felt safer since Guatemala. Maybe I've changed. Guns don't freak me out anymore and I've realized that poor populations do not imply a greater inherent risk to my safety. My worries over food, gas and shelter are gone. Everything works itself out in the end.

If I started this journey in Colombia I would have felt in danger and thought people were out to get me. But nothing in Colombia has changed from when I set out in the beginning. It would have all been in my head.

As I leave Colombia I remind myself of what I told myself before I crossed into Mexico:

"Quiet the voices of those who've never been and listen to those that have. You're going to be fine."

I am going to be fine and for the first time I truly believe it.

# DAY 148
# TULCAN, ECUADOR

"The mountains are calling and I must go."

John Muir

Latitude:    000° 48' 42" N
Longitude: 077° 43' 07" W

7,663 miles to Ushuaia

---

After another border crossing I transform from a foreigner in one land to another, this time in Ecuador. Everything is new and familiar at the same time. The land, people and currency change in an instant, but with my foreign eyes this constant flux is a standard in an ever-changing landscape. My constant motion makes it difficult to find familiarity and so everything has an otherworldly quality.

I spend a few days in Tulcan to fix up Jenny before we head into the Andes mountain range in Peru. I find a cheap hotel and a mechanic.

During my time in Tulcan I walk around the city. My gait is relaxed, my head is high, and my eye wanders where it wants. I look at passersby in the eye, and smile when I feel it's warranted. My smile is returned in kind more often than not. The anxieties of my past are gone. My environment is not something I approach with a guarded stance anymore.

Two days later Jenny's bald rear tire is replaced, grimy oil is swapped with a fresh batch, and the broken brake light bulbs shine for the first time in a month.

I notice a policeman on a newer model KLR, just like Jenny. I slow down to check out his modifications. His head darts towards me and he seems interested in me as well. He slows down and I pass. Minutes later five policemen on KLRs are riding next to me in formation. They are looking at me and I wave. They box me in and decelerate until we're all stopped.

"We have the same bikes!" I say.

They are not as excited about this as I am. It's a routine check of my papers and I'm all smiles as I'm preoccupied with the sight of five shiny KLRs. Their work is done, but I'm still talking bikes with them. One by one they start walking away, disinterested with my obsession. The tables turn and now I'm chasing cops away.

I continue southbound and don't see a toilet seat for the next two weeks. I haven't paid for a nice enough place that has them. Piles of used toilet paper gather next to toilets. The pipes can't handle paper.

Ecuador is filled with long days in the saddle, eating up the miles in the valleys. I'm headed for the heart of the Andes, which will be high altitude, winding roads that will slow my pace considerably. The crossing out of Ecuador and into Peru is quick and free of difficulties. The gas stations grow so sparse, I am forced to go to the nearest sign of civilization. I pass the village but see no gas station. I am miles from the village and there's no sign of anything else out here. I return to take a closer look on foot. I can walk the length of the village in minutes. In my big red suit, like Santa, I clomp down the dirt road looking for signs of gas. There are three-wheeled cabs and 50cc motorcycles putting around, so there must be something nearby. I ask a woman if she knows where I can find gas. She takes a guarded stance and shakes her head no. I step away smiling and apologizing for the intrusion.

A little boy is staring at me like I am an alien and I ask him the same question. He points down the road so I continue walking. A group of men are gathered around a table in the open air and I ask them as well. They have answers, welcoming handshakes and slaps of congratulations upon my back after they hear how far I have traveled. The gas station is a drum of gasoline and Jenny is plugged with a giant funnel in preparation for her fill up. The attendant drapes a rag over the funnel to filter particulates and pours two liter allotments until the tank is full. These are the conditions in the valley and I wonder what lies ahead among the mountain peaks.

I am headed to Machu Picchu. I can take the main roads along the lowlands then jut over to Cusco to take a train there, but main roads are boring and trading Jenny for a set of tracks is even worse than a car as far as the travel experience is concerned. Plus I get to dive into the Andes mountain range. They've been a chain of bumps on a wall map for two years and now I get to conquer them with Jenny. I've always wondered how Jenny would do at altitude. She's been up to 10,000 feet without a problem in the thin air, but there are 15,000 foot passes and I fear she'll choke to death. If anything does happen it will get progressively worse as I climb, so I'll have to be cognizant of Jenny's performance.

I turn away from the coastal highway that can deliver me to Machu Picchu in three days, but I dive into the Andes for a route I anticipate will take a week, I think. It's slow going up the slopes, a welcoming pace after the hurry in Ecuador. The vegetation dwindles as Jenny and I rise in elevation. The thinner the air, the less life it can support. It's these kind of conditions in which I feel the most alive. My bearing is south but an enormous mountain is towering in the east. I'm too curious and at the next intersection I take a detour towards it that adds 60 miles.

Jenny and I are at 10,000 feet and the mountain feels double that. The road winds around the peak and we climb another 3,000 feet. The cold is unbearable and with every blink my eyelids deliver a cold swipe against my eyes. It's time to turn on my electric vest and heated grips. I check my volt meter to see if my heated gear is draining the battery. The dial reads 10.5 volts. Anything under 11 volts means there is more electricity being drawn than she is generating. I turn off my heated grips and the meter jumps to 11.6 volts. The slope increases and Jenny's speed decreases under the strain of gravity and lack of oxygen. I check the meter and it reads 10.7 volts. I tune my heated vest down and the meter jumps up to 11.1 volts.

A cross wind blows Jenny to the edge of the road and brings us to what feels like a standstill. Like a bicyclist in a headwind, but with 37 horsepower instead. The landscape is barren and alien. There isn't a speck of green in sight and in a small section of land in Peru, I feel like I'm riding on the Martian surface. The rocky landscape extends as far as I can see, and for a moment I feel like the last person on Earth.

I circle around the peak that drew me here. I am close to the base and it stands looming over me. This peak is one of hundreds I have before me in my route to Machu Picchu.

The cold is slowly creeping through my many layers, and my hands are numb. My heated vest is binary in operation. I turn it on and watch my voltage meter fall to 11 volts. I turn it off and it slowly climbs back to a healthy 12.2 volts. Like a boiling kettle I watch the meter until I can start the cycle over and warm my bones.

I return to my original course and it's not long before Jenny and I are climbing another steep slope. This one is so taxing I have to kill the power to my vest. Jenny won't pull more than 20 MPH and the uphill switchbacks don't allow me to go much faster anyways. My eyes dart to the elevation reading on my GPS. An hour ago it read 13,000 feet, and I just passed 14,000 without the slope letting up. The next town is 40 miles beyond my range, and I wonder how I'll figure this one out. There's nothing I can do but to continue riding and see what happens. There's no use in worrying, but I picture myself coasting down the other end of this never ending mountain pass, engine off, finding every excuse not to hit the brakes.

My GPS reads 14,600 feet and signs of the highest point are in the distance. The road curls back and forth like a snake. My eyes watch the count:

14,700

14,800

14,900

I reach the pass and pause to take a picture of the readout at 14,975 feet. I am twenty-five feet shy of 15,000 feet. I'll round up when I tell others. It's easier to say anyways.

At the pass is a shed with a sign advertising the sale of gas. An old woman pours a gallon into Jenny to ensure we'll make it to the next station. A little boy, eight years old, plays with a cat. There is nothing but a simple stone structure they live or work from. Atop the world the boy stomps in puddles that litter the mountain pass.

Jenny is still choking on the thin air, but now she doesn't have to do it uphill. We begin our descent and most of the time she's idling. I'm just trying to keep her warm and I hold in the clutch to glide down the slopes on gravity. The road is a tangled mess of switchbacks that are fun to negotiate even at 10 MPH. I kill the engine and listen to the crisp wind howl against my helmet.

This is the highest mountain pass I've ever crossed and I'm surprised to see a green valley on the other side of it. Something is out of place, but I don't know what. There are white strands in the distance hanging on either sides of the valley. Around the next bend a huge waterfall comes into view. I come across them every 20 minutes. Drainage pipes are dug under the road to prevent the runoff from destroying the road.

Dozens of waterfalls later I start to notice what was missing back at the pass: a river. They are created from the runoff of water higher up. Throughout mountainous roads there's always one nearby, but this time there was no place higher up. The vast width of the valley allows me to see all the waterfalls converging. A thin dark line in the center of the valley weaves its way back and forth. Over the next few hours the line grows thicker and tiny signs of white water emerge. I descend as far as I can for the day to around 10,000 feet, and the stream turns into a raging river. It's not everyday you get to see the birth of such an awesome force.

Jenny is losing more power every day. It will take me a couple extra days at this pace but, whatever, I'm having a great time spending my day staring at peaks and valleys. Flamingos congregate near mile high lakes and llamas graze on bits of grass poking out between the rocks of a seemingly lifeless landscape.

I see a girl in the distance. She must be eight years old, ten tops. She's alone and walking behind a flock of sheep. She wields a strap and slings rocks at the straying sheep to keep them in line. From 50 feet away she strikes within feet of a stray and it scurries back in line. I wave as I pass and her arms drop to her side as she just stares back. I must look like an alien to her.

It's so cold I have my heated vest cranked up all the way, but I'm still shivering. This little girl is out here without much more than a few layers and a scarf lightly wrapped around her head. I wonder how an amazing girl like this turns out later in life, having so much independence and responsibility early in life.

---

One of my favorite movies is *Cast Away*. It's the story of a man stranded on a desert island for five years. I've always been fascinated by solitude and what it does to a person. I spend a lot of time alone so I'm a living example of it. This whole trip is a kind of desert island for me, except the ever-changing scenery that develops. What I love most about the story is the relationship between the main character and a volleyball. He calls it Wilson, after its manufacturer, and even paints a face on it to anthropomorphize it. As the days go on the relationship between Jenny and I becomes stronger and more weird. As I move through the land her handlebars in my lower peripheral vision are the only things that stay the same in a constantly changing landscape, and this comforts me.

In the depths of the Andes where things have grown more remote than I've ever experienced, my mind is pushed into strange places. I see a llama in the wild for the first time:

"Oh my god! Jenny! Jenny, did you see that?!"

There's no answer, and an answer isn't necessary. She's didn't have to see it. All that matters is that she's there with me when it happened. She's been there for everything. We lumber up a steep mountain grade and I check the altimeter on my GPS.

"I dunno, girl, we're pretty high. How are you doing?"

She keeps losing power.

"I think we're going to make it. I'm sorry. I should have changed out your main jet."

Her single cylinder keeps thumping away and it misfires every now and then.

"You're fine. You can do this. I gotta push your revs a little higher to burn up that unspent fuel. You're going to get the works when we hit the next major town. I'll get ya some fresh oil, we'll check on that fork seal I've been putting off. Just hang in there."

We have our squabbles. I push her to limits she can't take. She bites back and falls on me. She's good company. I have someone to care for. She's always there for me.

Jenny is getting worse as we climb higher and she completely stalls on a hill. I have to rev the engine high enough so that the excess fuel that isn't being burnt doesn't flood the engine. The power she's putting out on some hills barely keep us moving and I paddle along with my feet over the rocks.

There is a fork in the road and I stop to consider my options. The road to the left will lead me further into the Andes. I've been blown away by what I've seen already and want to continue. The road to the right leads to the coast where Jenny can run over 30 MPH at sea level. The elevations will only be getting higher, and if Jenny isn't running well now, a breakdown later is inevitable. I sit on the side of the road for an hour to think. I need to face the reality of the situation. I need to listen to Jenny.

I turn my back on the Andes and take a right to head for the coast. I'm taking the easier path and it's tearing me up inside. I feel like a coward for turning away from the challenge and an idiot for not expecting the effect of altitude on Jenny.

An hour later Jenny's carburetor is so dirty she won't fire anymore. I made the right decision at the fork, but either way I am in the same situation. Daylight is fading, so I start looking for places to camp. I will flag down a truck in the morning. A nearby mine generates a lot of traffic, especially with heavy trucks, so I'm not worried about finding a way out for Jenny.

I see a small house in the distance and walk towards it. I ask the owners if it is ok for me to camp on their land and they insist I sleep near their home to be safe. I roll Jenny down the road and set up camp just in time for sunset.

A truck stops and the woman explains my predicament. The driver says he can take me now, and I take up his offer. It's better than waiting on the side of the road tomorrow. I quickly pack up my tent and we throw Jenny in the back of his covered flatbed truck.

Jenny is tied down with a dozen rubber fan belts, but she's bouncing around a lot. It's 200 miles to the coast on these bumpy roads and the drivers says it will take five hours. Exhausted, I stay up to keep an eye on Jenny as she takes a beating in the back of the truck.

After two hours of fretting over Jenny like a first-time mother does over her child, I let her go. My helmet doubles as a great pillow so I put it on and shut the visor. To keep from rolling around I wedge myself between my luggage and a wall. I'm a deep sleeper.

It's hard for me to wake up in the morning. It's not that I'm not a morning person. I have an incredible ability to avoid moving from the place where I am sleeping. Over the years I've escalated my wake up techniques. I moved the alarm clock across the room, then added two. I got wise to snoozing these in my sleep though. I bought an alarm with wheels that rolls off my bedside table, forcing me to chase it around the room, but it wasn't long before I was showing up late for work and being reprimanded. Then there was the clock with an 80 decibel alarm, 20 shy of damaging your eardrums. That resulted in short bursts of panic which caused me to smash the clock while I tried to snooze in a frenzy. My latest alarm works best which forces me to perform algebra to snooze, but I keep getting better at math and it's just buying me time. We arrive in a coastal city and I wake up to the driver kicking my boots.

"Let's go, we're here!" he shouts.

It takes me a full minute to realize what is happening. There are three Peruvian men shouting at me and unloading Jenny onto the street. I have no idea where I am. After a week in the Andes, a city looks foreign to me. Had the Andes been a big dream? Is this a dream?

The driver asks $30 for the ride and I pay it without bargaining. He drops my luggage next to me, and I rub my eyes in a sleepy daze.

"Are you ok?" he asks.

"Yea...yea I'll be fine. Thanks again." I say.

He points to a hotel, and slaps me on the back before he drives off. In the morning I find a motorcycle shop to take a look at Jenny. She isn't even starting at sea level. He cleans out her carburetor and she's back to normal. The jet that lets air into the engine is too small for higher altitudes. I need to get a bigger one that will let in more oxygen when the air gets thin. He doesn't have any, but a city further south does. I head towards Trujillo to get Jenny a proper jet. I will be heading back into the Andes and this all will happen again if I don't do anything about it.

I find a Kawasaki shop that's like a high tech laboratory where mechanics wear clean white jumpsuits. The floors and concrete walls are glossy clean. I tell them what happened and they say it's no big deal to fix. The part only costs $15. I stick around to watch them dissect my carburetor in case I need to do this myself one day. I have the works done on Jenny. I'll be heading into Bolivia next and a breakdown there could be much more difficult to resolve.

My next stop is Machu Picchu. The tourism factor is pretty high. I could spend a month's worth of my budget for a few days there, so I try and skirt all the accommodations. I hear of a town nearby, Santa Marta, where you can walk to Machu Picchu. There's a squiggly line on my GPS that digs through the mountains. It looks off the beaten path so I head for it. I pass through the town of Nazca and south of it are the lines of the same name.

The road to Santa Marta is a one lane dirt track. I only see two other cars after eight hours of riding. I descend on a small town that isn't indicated on the map. My arrival is noticed by many and people start chatting with me.

I tell them I am heading for Santa Marta and they start laughing. Apparently the road I picked is too much off the beaten path so they tell me it takes eight days to make it there, and it's a footpath; motorcycles can't traverse it.

I've spent a day heading towards this dead end, but it doesn't damage my spirits. The ride was amazing and the thought of heading out the way I came isn't such a bad thing.

I know I won't make it out before nightfall so I take my time and have a late lunch in town. Kids follow me and peek over my shoulder as I map out the next few days on my GPS. I zoom in and out to show them where their village is and where I am from. Very soon they take control of the GPS and they are zooming around the map. I find geography to be a very powerful thing and the bright smiles from the kids as they explore their country are proof.

I backtrack a couple hours to the main road. I start to look for camping spots far from the main road. The terrain is too rugged and the cliffs too sheer. Finding a spot 100 feet off a road that's in the middle of nowhere seems a little excessive. I stake my tent in a dirt pull off and sleep among the clouds for the night.

Taking a train is the easiest way to cut through the mountains to the summit. After six months of spending my days in the saddle of a motorcycle the option sounds utterly boring and the price is outrageous. I decide to ride Jenny there, and it takes five hours to go 100 miles. I have 40 miles to go before I am stopped by a construction worker blocking the road. Apparently there has been a landslide and the road is out. Another dead end. I take a break to regroup and talk to the construction worker.

"What road can I take to reach Machu Picchu?" I ask.
"It is impossible, the road is out." she says.
"I know but there must be some other road."
"It is very long and dangerous."
"That's fine. I like those."

She looks at me confused.

"It is impossible."
"Wait, but you just said there was a road."

She's a dead end too. She's not helping me so I decide to head back. A cop shows up before I leave and he reiterates the construction worker's story. The road is closed and it is impossible to get to Machu Picchu by vehicle. I wonder why the cop was called in the first place since I was about to leave. I must have rattled the construction worker. Maybe I was yelling? I do that sometimes after the wind has been blasting through my ears for hours.

I have been fantasizing about parking Jenny atop Machu Picchu and damn it I was going to make it there with her. It's not about just getting there, it's getting there with Jenny. She deserves this! I've spent three days trying to reach the summit with Jenny only to hit dead ends. I have to ask one more thing before I leave even though I know the answer.

"How bad is the landslide? Maybe a motorcycle can get across?"

The cops' expression is answer enough.

I think I've exerted enough effort to get Jenny to Machu Picchu, but I still feel defeated. I turn around and go back to the town of Chinchero where I can take a train to the summit. The price is a fraction of the train from Cusco. Funds are running low and I measured everything in terms of gas tanks. The train ride costs me four gas tanks, normally about 800 miles by motorcycle, but by train it's only 40.

It takes three hours of wonderful backtracking to reach Chinchero. It's hard to find a cheap place to stay for the night and no one likes my proposition to camp in their parking lot. The cheapest place I can find is six gas tanks a night.

I find a building that looks like a hotel, but doesn't have a sign. The front of the building is a small convenience store. I ask about a room for the night and the man behind the counter checks with someone in the back. A woman comes out and looks me up and down. She says it would cost half a gas tank a night. I eagerly accept and they open up the gate for me to park Jenny. She will be safe while I am away for the day tomorrow at the summit. The man shows me to my room at the end of the two story building that has about 30 rooms.

He tells me his brother is out of town and that I can stay here. I realize this isn't a hotel at all. It's just a big house for family, with five generations living under the same roof. Dozens of cars are parked in the grassy lot. I see grandparents playing with grandchildren, maybe great grandchildren and then there's me.

My budget has forced me to take extra steps to get food, sleep and shelter. I wouldn't have been in this amazing home if it wasn't for my lack of affluence. This has been a running pattern and strangely I'm thankful for not having very much. The wisdom of "less is more", resonates with me in a way it never had before.

I make it to Machu Picchu and it's amazing. I soak in the surroundings, but my mind is already wondering about the next leg of the journey. It's destinations likes these that let me rest, and I'm a little detached from my surroundings, as wonderful as they are. Destinations worry me a little. They are an endpoint and I'm not comfortable standing still. The real adventure is on the road between the points and before I know it I'm on the road to Puno, the gateway to Bolivia where I fear and hope my greatest struggles are to come.

# DAY 170
# THE BOLIVIAN BORDER

"Chaos was the law of nature;
Order was the dream of man."

Henry Adams

Latitude:    016° 33' 49" S
Longitude: 069° 02' 11" W

4,883 miles to Ushuaia

---

The gateway to Bolivia is through Puno and bends around Lake Titicaca, the highest lake in the world where large commercial boats can navigate it. I arrive in Puno with two hours before sunset. There is a lot of commotion going on and it's hard to navigate through bustling crowds and double parked cars. I find out there's an annual festival where people throughout all of Peru travel to see it, and it's tomorrow. I'm willing to pay anything for a room, but everything is booked. After a long day on the road my patience is short and I'm visibly frustrated. Passersby look at me with concern. I look like a mess, and the tourists are afraid of me as I mutter curses under my breath.

"The goddamn annual festival just had to be tomorrow. Fuck. Son of a BITCH. Mother FUC--"

I attempt a U-turn on a hill that makes the streets of San Francisco look flat and I topple over Jenny in the middle of the streets.

"FUCK THIS!" I conclude and I am off to find a place to camp outside the busy streets of Puno.

The sun has set by now and I'm 30 miles out of the city where I have calmed down. The inky night closes in around me and I realize my headlight is out. I laugh it off and ride with my hazards on. They light up the road surprisingly well but there are a few close calls with cattle and dogs.

"Never ride at night Bill," I sigh.

I find a roadside motel with a broken sign. They have a room available, but $20 is too steep for me. Just an hour ago I was willing to pay $100, but I see a backyard with livestock and I think I can manage a camping spot instead. The hotel owner is confused by my request but entertains it anyways. He shows me to a storage closet with concrete floors and a tin roof. There's rusty nails waiting to snag you and hooks and chains hanging from the rafters.

"Perfecto!" I exclaim.

They drag in a straw mattress, a couple thick blankets, and it just cost me $5 for the night.

In the morning I pass Lake Titicaca and it's overwhelmingly unimpressive. It's just a lake like hundreds I've seen before. This one happens to be really high. This feat isn't impressive to the senses, and I probably had more enjoyment reading about it than actually seeing it.

Jenny and I limp our way to the border at 30 MPH. The slow pace doesn't bother me anymore. I would be fuming with anger in my former life, but I've adopted a more laid back attitude. "We'll get there when we get there", I tell myself. Vans pass me every few minutes in both directions. The roofs are piled with cargo and stuffed with people. Most are heading to the border to sell their wares to people crossing into Peru from Bolivia. I've seen it at every border and were this a week-long vacation I would pick up some trinkets, but my lack of storage space limits me. I arrive at the border town of

Desaguadero where vans are parked and men shout "Puno! Puno! Puno!" to advertise an open slot on a van back to town. People pack up and squish in for the three hour ride back home.

I arrive in the afternoon since the three hour ride took me five. Bolivia is one of the poorest countries in South America and I expect the border crossing to take some time. I feel like the area is safe, and that's enough for me to ignore my rule about staying near border crossings. Seven bucks gets me a small room with concrete walls and a tiny squeaky bed. I love hooks to hang things and there are a dozen of them. I can see exactly where everything is and it saves me a lot of time and worry. I hang my helmet, motorcycle suit, boots, jacket, water supply, scarf, and tank bag. My bag of bulky camping supplies sits neatly atop my two luggage cases. I've done this at least a hundred times by now and have grown more methodical. Everything is in its place for the next nine hours until I pack it all up and repeat the process tomorrow in Bolivia.

I arrive at the Peruvian immigration office. The export process goes smoothly but I learn that a Bolivian visa costs $125 and I am short. Before I left Puno I asked if there was a bank at the border and I got three confirmations that there was. I typically ask three different people the same question before I believe it to be true. The signs outside town indicated the presence of a bank nearby too, I just have to find it. A border guard, the hotel clerk, and a merchant all point to the Bolivian border when I ask about the bank. I get the exit stamp for Jenny and head to the Bolivian immigration offices.

I ask a border official, a restaurant owner and a bicyclist where the bank is and they all point to the Peruvian border.

Am I the target of some kind of joke?

I leave Jenny at the immigration office and walk back to Peru to make sure I'm not crazy. I ask three new people and they all tell me the bank is over in Bolivia. I return to Bolivia and everyone is telling me the bank is in Peru. Each side is holding the same delusion about the other. I kneel down, interlace my hands behind my head and squeeze my skull between my forearms until my face is red and my veins are popping out my arms like snakes. I curse under my breath through clenched teeth and in a minute my temper tantrum is over. I put my helmet on and a short maniacal laugh erupts as I realize what I have to do next. I have to return to Puno to get cash in order to enter Bolivia. I return to the Peruvian border to start the process of re-entering the country I just left an hour ago. A immigration official recognizes me and is curious.

"What happened?" he asks.

"I don't have enough money for the visa", I reply.

"Did you try the bank over there?" he points to Bolivia like everyone else.

"There is no bank", I said with a sigh.

"No, no, no. There is!" he insists.

We go back and forth on this point and I do all I can to not lose my shit. He shrugs, shakes his head and stamps my passport. Jenny is in no shape to go to Puno and back so I book a room at the place I stayed the previous night. I stow Jenny in a safe place and drop my gear in flurry of chaos. I follow the sounds of men shouting, "Puno! Puno! Puno!" and hop in a van. Three hours later I'm in Puno. I walk for ten minutes until I find an ATM and withdraw a lot of cash. There's no schedule for when vans arrive or leave for the border, but there is never a shortage of them. I head back to the border and pass Lake Titicaca for a fourth time. It's just as unimpressive as the first time from this vantage point. It cost me six hours for being $30 short. I have six weeks and 5,000 miles to go before I reach Ushuaia. The terrain is only going to get worse from here and I can't be wasting days like this anymore.

---

I circle the maze of streets that lead to the center of Bolivia's capital, La Paz. Vans like the one I took to Puno go wherever they like and swarm around me as I try and navigate. Normally I can squeeze between vehicles but there isn't enough room. A teenage boy leans outside the sliding door of a van and advertises the route while people jump on and off. The traffic gets heavier so I know I am getting closer to the city center. At an intersection I find myself in the middle of a deadlock triangle. Three huge yellow school buses are trying to move, but each of them is blocking the other. The children hang out the windows to point, smile and laugh at me. I make funny faces at them and the drivers keep on honking. Five minutes later one of the drivers finally reverses and we're all on our way. I come across more buses parked in the middle of intersections with blockades around them. Some protests are going on, but I'm not sure what about. I flash a smile and wave to the guys guarding the barricade. They return the warmth with an even bigger smile and wave me along. I splurge and pay $20 a night at a hotel near the center square. After sunset fireworks are going off in all directions around me and the people are marching and chanting something. I'm not sure if it's a celebration or a revolution. I'm too tired for either one and hit the sack.

Jenny is in bad shape, but luckily there is a Kawasaki dealer in town. Her carburetor is gunked up again from the altitude. Cleaning it only addressed the symptom, not the root of the problem. Because the air is thinner at higher altitudes I need a larger jet that lets more air into the engine. I get lost finding it and they are closed for the standard three hour afternoon lunch and siesta. I have nowhere else to go so I get comfy on the sidewalk and read a book. I finished Kerouac's *On The Road* last month, and now I'm on his earlier work, *The Dharma Bums*. I am jarred awake by the opening of the steel gate I am leaning against. The Dharma put me to sleep and now I turned into just a plain old bum.

The shop is amazing. The mechanics walk around in spotless white overalls on glossy floors. Jenny and I look like what the cat dragged in and I feel like I'm traipsing dirt through my grandmother's home. They diagnose my problem quickly and have my carburetor dissected on a bench within the hour. The replacement jet costs $15 and I kick myself for not anticipating this while I was back home. I knew this would happen, but my "let's see what happens" attitude kept me pushing Jenny to her limits and getting us stranded in the Andes.

On the other hand, if I did have that two ounce piece of metal with me I would have simply continued on my way without having met the people who took me in, and the man who hauled Jenny and me through the dark for five hours. I've already forgotten the solitary miles it took to get us where we broke down, but I'll never forget the people that helped us. Mechanical failures have been some of the best things that happen to me even though I fear it like the plague. I'm good at being completely independent. Too good really, but Jenny has her way of knocking me on my ass (literally at times) to make a point: "Slow down dummy! You're on an adventure of a lifetime and you're passing everything up." Someone said behind every great man is an ever greater woman. I'm no great man, perhaps because my primary feminine relationship is with a personified hunk of metal. The road does weird things to me.

Jenny is fixed and I have rested enough. We're off to the Salar de Uyuni, the world's largest salt flat. You can ride over the wide expanse of white nothingness in the dry season, and in the wet season a thin pool of water reflects the sky like a mirror. I don't know what season it is right now, but I'll find out in a few days.

I exit my hotel to find the street has turned into a bustling market. Dark bronze women are hauling enormous weights on their backs. They strategically bundle their products into a large blanket and hold it together with carefully placed ropes. One or two braids from their thick black hair peek out under their bowler hats. I ask if they could make some room for Jenny and they don't look happy. I'd be pissed too if I had to move all that stuff again after carrying it up the steep hills from however far they came. A man pulls me aside and tells that things will settle down in a few hours and I should try exiting then.

Things are less hectic but the women give me just as much grief when I ask them if I can pass through. I fire up Jenny and squeeze my way through repeating, "Sorry! Sorry!" over and over. Women cover their ears and the others wave their arms at me in a "get out of here!" motion. Our thorns are out of each other's sides in two minutes and I start looking for the southern exit of La Paz. A few hours later I've made it and I stop for coffee and plan my route to the Salar de Uyuni. I study my Spanish dictionary and smirk as I stumble upon the word "paz." It means "peace" and I realize that La Paz literally means "The Peace."

---

Early in the day I spot a welder in a small town. They are easy to find because they work out in the open for all the traffic to be blinded by their spark. My luggage rack is broken in a critical area that causes it to sag closer and closer to my chain. He starts working right away. Sparks shower over my rear tire and his son uses a soda bottle with a small hole in the cap as a squirt bottle to cool down parts of the metal. Jenny hisses and steam rises up from her rear tire. It takes 10 minutes and $3 before I am back on the road.

I am heading for Salinas de Garci Mendoza, a town north of the Salar de Uyuni. There's nothing special about it other than its position relative to the salt flat. It sets me up to bisect the salt flat and give me the maximum amount of isolation possible. After all this solo riding I am still searching for a greater degree of solitude. I have it all planned out, too. I heard a story on a radio program that explained what it was like to be blind. At least it tried to give it a shot. Since then I have wondered what it would be like to be blind and I decided that the Salar de Uyuni would be the prime place for this experiment.

I would camp in the middle of the vast salt flat and wear a blindfold for as many days as I could stand it. The main characteristics I like about the salt flat is its wide open spaces, lack of people and not much to trip over. I have a spool of fishing line so I can tie one end to Jenny and then go for walks without getting lost. Cooking meals will be tricky, but that's the point. I wanted to go through the challenges that blind people face. I want to stumble a few miles in their scuffed up shoes.

Some muddy fields gave Jenny and me some problems. The road was closed off and the only bypass is through these fields. Large trucks and even a double decker bus plow through the maze of tracks. The trail is constantly forking to the left due to flooding until I'm not pointed anywhere near the original road. I find a "shortcut" that gets Jenny stuck deep into the mud. A van filled with men give me a hand and they motion to the dry part of the field with a confused look.

"Why did you drive through the mud?" they ask.

I throw my hands up in the air, "I'm an idiot."

I learn my lesson and don't bother looking for any more shortcuts through the muddy mess. The pavement ends and the road conditions worsen. Post holes are not obstacles anymore and I test the limits of Jenny. I am launching over them at 40 MPH and the rear shock absorbs the brunt of the force. After a couple hours I feel my confidence on the dirt improving. Ahead is a subtle fork in the road. I can veer to the right and climb a dodgy hill or stay straight. I follow my mantra in these situations:

When in doubt, stay straight.

The road dips suddenly, we go airborne, and a queasy feeling erupts in the pit of my stomach. Milliseconds later shockwaves reverberate through Jenny's front forks, into the handlebars and into my body. At 40 MPH Jenny bottoms out. Friction is a force I take for granted until it is gone.

Everything happens so fast as it always does. Jenny falls to the left and then bounces back to land on her right side. I am with her for the first fall, then topple to the left and slide along the rocks. My left knee is throbbing and I can barely walk on it. My right hand is being squeezed in a vice of fluids, rushing to the areas of trauma. A bus I passed minutes before catches up with me. They see the whole thing. The driver rushes to my aid and says something, but my mind is blinded with pain as I roll on the ground. My chest is pumping, and my breathing is rapid. Each breath is a second apart and without control I let out a yell over and over. It's not a scream like from a wounded soldier in a movie. It's like what you do when the doctor asks you to say "ah", but at the top of my lungs.

AAAAAH!
AAAAAH!
AAAAAH!

I am clutching my hand and rolling back and forth on the ground. I grip at my glove to take it off and a man helps me get it off. It slips off and a gut curdling cry comes out as tears pour out my eyes. My thumb is broken, but I don't know it. I've never broken a bone before and I think broken bones are completely debilitating and make your body shut down. I haven't shut down, so I must not have broken anything and I'll go on believing it's a sprain for the next month.

The men are asking how I am but I don't know. I ignore them and limp over to Jenny. I extend her kickstand and pull her up off the ground with the help of the other men. They are asking about my well-being while I am inspecting Jenny's. They keep badgering me, so I strip off my suit and inspect myself. Adrenaline can hide some nasty stuff so a visual check is always a good idea. Everything seems OK. The bus driver and passengers get back in the vehicle and go on their way. They point me to a town a kilometer away where I can get help.

I assess Jenny's damage. There is a big oil stain under her. She is hemorrhaging and I quickly find the source. The right side crank case has been ruptured from the crash. The water pump has a hole in it as well. No oil. No coolant.

I consider the idea of pushing Jenny to the town in eye sight. I quickly dismiss the possibility after I survey the hills required to reach it. Jenny starts up like the bullet proof bitch she is. I keep the revs low and coast down the hills eventually killing the engine and riding gravity into the town.

The town has a population in the single digits. People gather around and I tell them my story. A wife looks irritated, and late for something. She doesn't care about my problems. Another man lets me camp in his yard so I can wait for a truck on the side of the road in the morning.

Ten thousand miles away Amber is refreshing her browser every five minutes. The web page displays my current coordinates. I have a personal locator beacon that logs my location and can be used to call for help in the event of an emergency. The dot on the map hasn't moved for hours. She switches to satellite view and there is nothing on the map that leads her to believe there is something worth stopping for. She knows something is wrong but doesn't know what. I could be taking a nap on the side of the road or dead, and I know which scenario she defaults to. Amber has already scolded me about these kinds of situations. When I am at a standstill in the middle of nowhere, I am to hit the "OK" button to let her know I am still alive. I pitch my tent and collapse inside of it. Pain is coursing through my body and I hit the "OK" button on the beacon.

---

I am told that I can find help for Jenny in the town of Challapata, 50 miles away. I get up before sunrise and sit along the road to flag down a truck to take us there. I am hoping for some traffic moving eastward, but everyone is heading west. The morning rush ends around ten o'clock. Only five vehicles pass by.

I grow tired of reading after a few hours. My knee is in bad shape. I can't put much weight on it so I go for a hobble to change the scenery. Like a wounded animal, my tracks in the dirt consist of a right boot print and a jagged line on the left where my busted leg drags. It's dry here, and I'll lose water just sitting still. I find some water settled in the center of a 50 foot crater. With this morning's traffic I prepare for the possibility of being here for days and gather enough water. I set a timer and force myself to take a big gulp of water every ten minutes despite my lethargy.

The lunch rush is less active than the morning. The first eastward vehicle approaches but it's a passenger car and worthless to me. It's two o'clock, hour nine, and my morale is getting worse. I force myself to remember all the trucks I had passed yesterday to convince myself that they weren't a figment of my imagination and what I am doing is the right choice. The wind picks up and my face is starting to get wind burned. I find some rocks and build up a small wall I can lay behind to escape the relentless wind. The sun is hanging low in the western sky with only a few hours of light left. I am convinced my ride won't arrive today, but lay on the road anyways to avoid the tortuous "what ifs" that would go through my mind if I left the road for even a minute.

I curl into a ball behind my wall and stare at my GPS, catching fleeting satellite signals. It triangulates my position and re-calculates every 10 seconds, changing only within yards. Slowly I zoom out, always with my position in view, and look at all the countries I've been through. This whole journey feels like a dream and I fear the end coming soon. I am stranded in the middle of nowhere with a broken motorcycle.

I zoom out wide enough to see home and my distance away from it. I have never felt so alone and isolated as I do at this very moment. I don't realize I'm crying until the wind changes direction and blows cold against the tear trails on my face. I'm too exhausted to quiver a lip and my face is expressionless. Maybe this is a brand of sadness and desperation that doesn't manifest itself in the ways I expect. Emotional intelligence was never my strong suit.

I switch to my locator beacon and stare at the random blinking of a light. I wonder what Amber is thinking back home. I told her to expect blackout periods in our communication here in Bolivia, and it's getting close to the 24 hour mark since she's seen me move from this area.

With my GPS and my locator beacon, both of us know where I am, at any moment. The numbers on my GPS tell me so:

19° 21' 19" S
67° 12' 44" W

It's the only piece of information that is being transmitted but I feel connected with it. I ensure to keep my batteries charged and swap old ones for new. It becomes company for me. I hit the "OK" button and pull my hat over my face as the next round of dust devils spin around me.

It's four o'clock and I hear a vehicle coming from the west. I don't get my hopes up until I verify it's a truck. It is, and I jump to my feet. All day I had been translating common sentences I need to ask the driver and writing them down. I rehearse them over and over.

"I need help."
"My motorcycle is broken."
"Can you drive me and my motorcycle to Challapata?"

The most important one:

"I have money."

They stop and I explain my situation. They are willing to help and we come to an agreement at $20. They waste no time, so I show them the way to Jenny. With a father, wife and two little ones in the truck cab, there is no room for me. I hang outside the truck using the step and grab onto the inside handle. They back the truck up to a dirt ramp and we push Jenny into the enclosed truck bed with ease. We butt Jenny against a wall and tie her down with long rubber straps that look like a fan belt. I sleep on some bags of rice for the bumpy two hour ride to Challapata.

It is dark by the time we arrive at the driver's home. My muscles are sore and starting to stiffen up from the crash. My energy has been sapped from sitting in the sun all day. He invites me into his home, but I apologize and ask if I could stay put and sleep in the back of his truck. He shrugs and shuts the cargo doors. No need for a tent tonight. I blow up my sleeping pad and collapse to sleep in my motorcycle suit with my hat pulled over my eyes.

In the morning the sun turns the cargo area into a greenhouse and I wake up sweating. I climb up and slip out through the tarp covering the truck. The driver takes me to the town welder, Chino. The punctures to Jenny's engine case are bad, and this is where I find out whether I can continue to Ushuaia or head home.

Chino is an older man, in his 50s with hands like stone and a smile of a saint. He's not a talker despite being one of the most popular men in town. People drive up and drop off mechanical parts for repair. Each time he studies the object without saying a word and after a few minutes he nods and sets it aside for later. He takes a look at Jenny and his cheeks puff up in an "oh boy..." kind of way. I ask him if he can fix her but he ignores me and starts taking her apart. Jenny's guts are exposed in a few minutes and Chino brings the damaged metal plate to his workbench for a closer look.

"How bad is it?"

"Bad," he bluntly states.

"Can you fix it?"

He nods then says, "But first, breakfast."

I am ecstatic. Too excited to eat and I sit and wait for Chino, my savior's return. There are two problems: a three inch fracture that caused my oil to drain and a caved in spot on the water pump, causing my coolant to leak. Chino moves slowly and deliberately to bend the metal back into place. I try and help, but feel like I am just getting in the way. He seals the water pump leak and puts down his tools. "Lunch," he says and walks away.

In my head I think, "Of course lunch. Whatever you like. Can I pick up the bill? Take your time Chino. You the man!" Chino returns and starts on the long fracture. It takes him four hours until he's ready to reassemble Jenny and see if there are signs of leaks. We fire up Jenny and I inadvertently hop up and down at the sound of her engine. Chino gives me a look that says, "Don't get too excited." He lets the engine run for 20 minutes. The only way to make sure the welds will hold is to see how it performs when the engine is hot. The temperature warning gauge flashes red.

Fuck.

Chino holds his finger up and examines Jenny. The coolant is starting to cycle through the radiator. He tops it off and the temperature light shuts off.

I thank him over and over and stop myself short of giving him a big hug. We start talking costs and Chino says, "$100?" with a sly grin. This is everyone's opening bid for almost anything. The truck driver started at $100 along with the other welder back in La Paz. Perhaps most foreigner's will pay it so that's why they try. I wince at the price then he counters with $20. I give him double and thank him again. Jenny is fixed, but I am still healing. I spend an extra day in Challapata to gather strength for another attempt to make it to Garcí Mendoza.

I could use more rest but I force myself back onto the road. There will be plenty of time for rest in the middle of the salt flat. I head down the familiar road to Salinas de Garcí Mendoza. I arrive at the muddy field where I got stuck three days ago. The trails had changed from the rainfall. What was a solid path before is now a muddy trap. Evidence of stuck vehicles are everywhere with grass and brush stuck deep in tire track ruts. It's the only way to gain traction. The trails cover the field like vines and leave me with the same question every 50 feet:

Left or right?

One path lets me move freely and the other leaves me stuck for an hour digging and grunting in the mud. At one point I find a third choice, a shortcut, but half of my front tire sinks into the soil after a few yards. Luckily a few people passing by help me out. Afterwards they direct me to the correct route and once I stop huffing and puffing I speak.

"I thought this way was better, but it's very bad."

They all erupt into laughter and return to their van.

The muddy field is behind me and I'm starting to make some real miles now. My engine cuts out like in Peru when my carburetor was choking on the thin air, but I had already fixed that problem with a new jet. With a bad knee I hobble up the hill to a village where a man helps me troubleshoot Jenny. He looks at my air filter and cringes.

"It's very dirty" he says.

It looks fine to me and I am skeptical about his diagnosis, but he insists so I follow his instructions. Nearby an old woman is selling plastic liters of soda. I buy one and start chugging it in front of her while she looks at me weird. I cut the bottle in half to siphon gas into and wash the air filter. We replace the clean air filter and Jenny roars to life. This guy knew the problem after listening to the engine run for only 30 seconds. It seems everyone in Bolivia is smarter than me.

The main road keeps forking and I follow my mantra in these situations:

When in doubt, stay straight.

I stay straight, assuming that the sharp forks will spit me out to the nearby farms. Eventually I am spat out onto the edge of the salt flat where the mud is dry and I can pick up speed. The scenery is stunning, and I am mesmerized by the pattern of shadows cast onto the dirt. It's not long before I notice a dark patch and before I know it Jenny and I are sliding across the muddy desert at 40 MPH. We hit a patch of slippery mud. My leg is pinned under Jenny and surrounded by the buildup of mud from the slide. I scream out in pain with short bursts of breath. My ankle is sprained and I've agitated my knee. I squirm out from under Jenny to pick her back up but it's impossible. I can't get a proper footing in this mud and my energy is sapped.

I abandon Jenny and start walking to a ridge I think is the main road. My mantra failed me and once again I feel like a fool. I plan on camping on the side of the road until I find help, but instead I stumble on a small village with seven houses. An old man, directs me to an old woman who directs me to a man who says he can help. We walk a mile into the muddy desert and lift Jenny. He directs me to a path that would get me back to the road. I ride through the muck with my heels dug in like skis as my rear tire fishtails left and right.

Jenny dies before I make it to the dry trail back to town. I diagnose all I can before I give up and start pushing. I stop every ten feet to catch my breath. It will take hours at this rate, so I walk back to town to ask of the man another favor. He is already walking towards me, realizing something is wrong since he hadn't heard my engine running. We begin pushing together, making good headway. After a while I stop to take breaks and I can tell the man is growing frustrated with my lack of endurance. After an hour we make it back to his house in town. I ask him how long he has lived here.

"60 years" he says.

Despite appearing to be 45 he turns out to be 60. He has lived here for his whole life in this town of seven homes in the middle of nowhere. It is a little embarrassing to find out this old man was kicking my butt as we were pushing the bike. I was always the one stopping for a break. This guy is as strong as an ox and twice my age.

He has to leave for the evening, and lets me camp in his yard. I have an hour of daylight so I sit on the side of the road to hail down trucks that might take me to Salinas de Garci Mendoza. The sun sets in the west and I spot a lone man walking down the road from the east. He approaches me, we trade greetings and he sits down to chat. He is also on his way to Salinas de Garci Mendoza, 20 miles from here. I tell him my predicament and he wonders if the driver of a truck I hail down can take him too. We pass the time by trading stories.

He speaks quickly and emphatically about everything. He is going to Mendoza to try and find his brother. He hands me a business card with his picture on it. He is carrying a plastic grocery bag filled with three empty water bottles, toothpaste, and a toothbrush with bristles worn down to the nub. He shows me the other members of his family from the bundle of business cards and coupons clippings. He shows me one after the other.

"How many brothers do you have?"

"120!" he says, smiling wide enough to reveal the remaining three teeth in his head.

I realize this guy is insane. I continue talking. The company is nice despite the lack of sanity. I recall myself crying behind some rocks on the side of the road the other day and all the mistakes that led to that moment. Perhaps I shouldn't be too judgmental. I finally flag down a truck. I begin explaining my predicament, all the while the vagabond is talking furiously behind me and making the couple in the truck nervous.

"I'm sorry, I don't know this person."

His madness is jeopardizing my ticket out of here and eventually he walks off, frustrated with the driver's harsh words that I don't understand. They are willing to haul my bike to Mendoza after we come to an agreement on price. They pull around to my bike, and just for kicks I try starting it and miraculously Jenny fires up! I am ecstatic.

"I'm good! I'm good! Thanks, but I don't need your help!"

I keep the engine running, gather my things and hit the road. On the way out of town I see the vagabond. I have been on the receiving end of so much kindness throughout this journey and I want to give back when I can. I pull up next to him.

"Wanna go?"

He smiles that gum filled smile and hops on the back with his arms around my waist. This guy is not going to find his imaginary brother in Mendoza, but he is going there anyways. Why not make it a little easier for him. It is tough riding with the extra weight of a passenger along with the dark void closing in around us.

"Just 20 miles," I keep thinking.

I look down at the odometer way too often, like watching a kettle boil. We approach a river that is wide and littered with boulders. Blasting through in a straight path is not an option. I ask the vagabond to get off since it will make it easier to cross. I plunge into the ice cold water, zigging and zagging and feeling the force of the water pushing against my boots. When hesitation starts to take over in situations like this that require boldness I scream at myself.

"GO! GO! GO! GIVE IT GAS! YOU GOT THIS! GO!"

I make it ten feet shy of the edge, and Jenny falls into the knee deep water. The vagabond and I can't pick it up. He hops out of the freezing water with his sandals and I keep trying. Minutes later a light illuminates the river as a huge truck approaches and plows through the crossing. They keep going despite my cries for help. A car coming from the opposite direction stops to help get Jenny upright, but now she isn't starting and we can't move forward. I wave the men away and thank them for their help.

With ice cold water flooding my boots I try and diagnose the problem as I keep Jenny balanced against the force of the water. The headlight is out, so it's probably a fuse. The vagabond's patience is gone and he's trying to get rides from the trucks that are passing by.

"Just give me five minutes!" I shout.

We just met, but I want him to stay. Luckily I kept my fuses close. I rip off Jenny's seat and throw it to dry land to access the fuse box. Minutes later I find my fuses, replaced them and Jenny roars back to life and onto dry land. Having no success at getting a ride, the vagabond is close, and I tell him to get back on Jenny.

We finally make it to Mendoza and the vagabond directs me to a place I can stay for the night. We spent a few hours together, but the intensity of those hours made me feel like we were lifelong friends. It's sad to see him go. He disappears down a dark street, in search for a brother he will never find.

I climb up a hill and find the hotel. The hospitable owner insists I eat, but I argue and tell him I am too tired. I hobble to my room to relax and record all of the events in my notebook so I won't forget. While taping my knee and ankle I hear a knock at the door. I open it up to find the owner with a tray of food I quickly scarf down.

I sleep for 14 hours and wake up refreshed. I grab a late lunch and ask the hotel owner if he recommends any areas in the salt flat for me to see. He pauses, and says that it's impossible to pass through the Salar de Uyuni due to the water. I rush outside to find the salt flat completely flooded. The muddy fields, the slippery desert and the river crossing were telling me the same thing: it's the wet season. But I hadn't given any thought to what the environment was telling me. I was too busy trying to conquer it.

A week full of crashes and injuries to Jenny and me leads me to a dead end. There's no other way to head south except the way I arrived. I start laughing hysterically at the irony of it all. I recollect the previous week and it feels like a month. I've lived more in that week than any other in my life, and I have no regrets despite the setback. The salt flat is a giant mirror leaving no distinction between the earth and sky. It's one of the most beautiful things I've seen. I spend three days healing and resting, then turn back the way I came.

I backtrack to the east side of the Uyuni. I've had enough adventure in Bolivia before I even reached the salt flat, and I'm looking forward to moving towards another milestone, the Chilean border. The highlands are wearing me out so I decide to take the first available route west to get over the Andes and closer to the Pacific. Things are slow going, but I've developed more patience here and I try and focus on the little things around me. Fluorescent green moss covers exposed rocks that litter the fields like mines. It looks like an alien landscape, but an occasional grazing llama snaps me back to reality. The dirt trail is growing more and more faint as the day goes on and I wonder if I'm headed for a dead end. I keep myself pointed towards the border crossing and hope for the best.

Chino's welding job is holding up, but there is a small leak and I am losing engine coolant. I have 200 miles to cover until I reach the border with nothing in between. The roads in Chile will improve so I just need to make it to the border before I stop to address the leak. I strap five gallons of water onto Jenny. Half is for me, and the other half is for her.

The washboard on the road is rattling my teeth loose and throwing the water bottles every which way. I secure the bottles but soon they make their way loose again. I take a look and realize the left luggage rack is in poor condition and is the source of all the rattling. My luggage racks have been nothing but trouble and I've welded and re-welded them over the past five months. I decide to reorganize my luggage setup. I move my left luggage case behind me on Jenny's passenger seat. Jenny is lopsided now and I have to keep her bars constantly turned to the left to counteract.

A couple hours later my rear tire starts to feel squishy and I stop to see what's going on. It's going flat. It's my second puncture since the one back in Minnesota, so I can't complain. Without too much trouble I replace it. The sun is hanging low in the sky so I get going to try and make it to the border by sunset.

Jenny is overheating more frequently and I have to stop every hour to refill her engine coolant reservoir that is slowly draining. I'm close to the border, just 50 miles away. I'm pouring water into Jenny's radiator as steam whooshes all around me, and I notice my tool tube missing. The last time I saw it was when I was repairing my flat, 40 miles ago according to my GPS. I am already pushing the limits of Jenny's range and I consider whether I can go back to look for it without running out of gas. I do the math in my head, then I double check it by writing it out. I can't be sure where it fell off, but I have just enough gas for me to make it to the border. Any backtracking will leave me stranded in this desert and I haven't seen another car all day. I want to go back, but I can't argue with the numbers.

"Fuck it."

My optimism assures me everything is going to be ok without my tools. I start recollecting what was in the tool tube and realize that I don't use the majority of the things I packed. I whittle down a list of tools I've used frequently and it comes out to about $40 worth. Everything is replaceable.

I arrive at the border and it's a ghost town. The sun is setting and all the offices are closed. There is a small town on the Chilean side, but there's nothing but an abandoned railroad station on the Bolivian side. I backtrack and find some hills in the distance to setup camp for the evening. Throughout the day I was drinking water sparingly since I didn't know how much worse Jenny's leak could have gotten. So I gorge on water knowing I can get more tomorrow.

A steady drip from her engine forms a puddle of water and I try to ignore it. There's nothing I can do about it until morning. I slip into my tent and sleeping bag without taking off my motorcycle suit. The temperatures are going to dip down low tonight and the extra insulation will help. I'm looking forward to easier days on the road in Chile, but can't help feeling sad to leave Bolivia. It's one of the most beautiful countries I've visited and the people's warmth has been so uplifting. I feel like I've seen so little, and imagine I will return here one day.

# DAY 181
# THE CHILEAN BORDER

"Once having traversed the threshold, the hero moves in a dream landscape of curiously fluid, ambiguous forms, where he must survive a succession of trials. This is a favorite phase of the myth-adventure."

The Hero With a Thousand Faces
by Joseph Campbell

Latitude:   021° 12' 47" S
Longitude: 068° 13' 46" W

4,096 miles to Ushuaia

---

I wake up shivering an hour before sunrise. Throughout the night I had slipped off my sleeping pad and my body was in contact with the ground. Despite the sleeping bag, motorcycle suit, and three layers, my body heat is sapped. The pliable protective pads around my knee, elbow and shoulder are solid from the cold. After a half hour my camp is packed away and I no longer feel like a robot with stiff joints walking around.

I am the first to arrive at the border. I dance the border crossing dance and exit Bolivia and enter Chile. The *thud* of the stamp on my passport always brings a smile to my face. Before leaving I crawl under Jenny to get a closer look at the engine coolant leak. I'm laying in the mud cranking wrenches and being a spectacle for a group of tourists on a double decker bus waiting to enter Bolivia. A man comes up and shows me an old remedy for these kinds of leaks. He tells me to take a bar of soap and mix it with sugar. It should create a thick goo that will harden and seal the leak temporarily. He finds the soap, and brings me a saucer of sugar. A few stray dogs steal a nip of sugar from me, and I shoo them away. The tourists are in line nearby and start protecting my sugar from the dogs for me. I rev Jenny up and with the heat the soap is holding to Jenny's engine.

I've been rough camping for the past week and I fantasize about a long hot shower in the next piece of civilization I come across. I have 150 miles before the next town and I'm chugging along on fumes through the alleys of the border town. There isn't a gas station here like I anticipated. I meet some Chileans passing into Bolivia in a two nicely outfitted trucks for their own adventure. They offer up some of their gas but we can't find a long enough hose. An immigration officer directs me to the police station, who directs me to a local municipal building, who points me to a small restaurant with a small convenience store at the front.

"Is it possible to buy gas here?"

"No, we only sell food here," the woman behind the counter says.

"I understand, but there are no gas stations here and I was told I could find some here."

"We only sell food here," she says with a blank face.

The conversation doesn't evolve much more until we are both visibly frustrated with each other, so I try a different approach.

"If I don't get gas, I can never leave this place. Is there any way for me to get gas from you or someone else?"

She pauses, and walks out of the room. Her husband returns and I tell him my situation. He looks me up and down, nods and motions me to follow him to the back of the building. He unlatches three locks on a large door, rolls it open to reveal a garage with tools covering the wall, and a large tank of gasoline. He fills up my tank as I thank him over and over.

Half way through the 150 miles to the next city the dirt turns to asphalt. The moment Jenny's front tire hits the smooth road I let out a sigh of relief, as if it was my first time on a road without bouncing around. We are floating on a cloud, but the party is short-lived when the orange temperature gauge turns on, and my heart sinks. The soap seal saved me an extra 50 miles, but eventually eroded away from the hot engine coolant. The coolant is pouring out in a solid stream. I spot a large nail on the side of the road.

"Fuck it."

With axe in hand I crawl under Jenny and pound the nail into the hole with the hope of slowing down the leak. Scrunched between the ground and Jenny's engine, I swing the butt of the axe against the nail's head awkwardly. The stream turns into a drip and I'm satisfied.

I arrive in Calama and survey the town. There's a large hardware store for me to replace my tools, a motorcycle shop and even a two story mall. I haven't seen a city this modern since Ecuador. I've been in the rough for so long the atmosphere feels strange. I notice a storefront displaying stainless steel cookware alongside a chainsaw and think, "that's more like it."

I find a cheap hotel on the edge of town and spend an hour washing the remnants of Bolivia off of me. In the evening I learn I had made a mistake converting the Chilean currency and the room costs $20 a night instead of the $7 I had thought. I'm not sure how many days I will need to stay until Jenny's coolant leak is fixed. I put the issue to rest and wait until I hear something from the mechanic tomorrow before I seek out cheaper accommodations.

I walk across town to the mechanic even though I'm still limping. I always like walking through the new towns I encounter. I can get a more personal look and feel of a city on foot. I keep noticing dogs everywhere, and they are friendly too. I sit down on a bench in the town square and the sleeping Labrador underneath me almost goes unnoticed. Sometimes there are packs that form in the streets and fights break out with outsiders. I keep watching and the outsider becomes a part of the group five minutes later.

For breakfast I browse the shops and buy fluffy pastries and coffee that isn't instant. I had just started getting used to gulping down the last grainy gulp of the instant coffee I had been drinking for the past month. At the motorcycle shop I take out my schematic of basic motorcycle parts with their appropriate Spanish names so I can talk to the mechanic. I'm afraid Chino's welding work isn't holding up and that coolant is mixing into the engine with the oil. A light grey sludge cakes the port hole on the engine case where the oil level is visible. It's not a good sign.

After inspection we find the shaft that spins a propeller to cycle coolant through the cooling system is broken and it explains the leak. Chino's welding is still rock solid. The manager can have the part shipped from Santiago and tells me it might arrive in two days or ten.

Back at the hotel I prepare for a ten day wait and try negotiating with the host. I explain my whole situation about the part from Santiago and we agree on $7 a night if I can set up my tent in the back of the hotel in a storage area on some gravel. I'm roughing it again, but it's a little harder to bear with all the luxuries in eyesight of my tent.

After my urban campsite is set up I head for the hardware store to replace my tools I left stranded in Bolivia. I've narrowed down all the wrench and socket sizes I absolutely need. I spend an hour drooling over all the tools, and after I'm done I've reduced the weight compared to my previous tool set by 20 pounds.

I look like a hobo with my ragged clothes and bushy beard. I feel like a circus act at the mall as I stroll down the long corridors and window shop. I used to be a mall rat as a teenager and being here always takes me back to those times. Rollerblading away from security guards, smoking used butts from the ash trays and trying to pass for 18 for R rated movies. I wonder what my younger self would think of me if he saw me now.

"Where the hell did I go wrong?" he would probably say.

Two days later I check in with the guy at the motorcycle shop and it turns out they can't have the part delivered. This kind of thing would normally enrage me. I would ask why they didn't realize this before, and emphasize how much time of mine they've wasted. But my demeanor is more chill and my expectations are lower. Most importantly, I realize bitching won't help my situation, so I ask for the nearest welder.

The welder is two miles away but Jenny's not operational so I will have to push her. I scout out the location on foot since the directions contain a landmark I "can not miss" which I usually always miss. "It's good exercise", I tell myself as I rationalize an extra 4 miles of walking. I make it back to the shop and start pushing Jenny. A mechanic I've been palling around with the past couple days comes and helps me push for the whole two miles despite my protest at the incredible generous hand he is lending.

At the welding shop I explain my problem. They exhibit some hesitation, but are happy to take my money and give it a try. The welder does his thing while I preoccupy myself with the dozens of nude calendars posted along the shop walls, the oldest which dates back to 1987. They are done quick and I am eager to test out their work. I grab the repaired part from his hand and start reassembling Jenny while they all watch. I flip through my service manual to double check my work.

1) Install water pump shaft and sprocket.
2) Line up clutch bolt.
3) Apply gasket grease to clutch plate
4) Tightened the 14 bolts evenly

I dump the oil in, fill up the reservoir and fire Jenny up. The guys cheer and slap me on the back, but my face is stone cold and not convinced yet. I need to see if she overheats when she gets up to operating temperature. For five minutes I rev the engine hard, and stick my head near the water pump to check for any noises. No sign of any leaks, but I still want to put it through some more tests. I take her out on the street until I'm satisfied and return to the shop with a big grin on my face. I walk up to everyone in the shop and shake their hand.

"Thank you! Thank you! Thank you!"

I even thank the guys that just watched. Jenny and I can continue our journey to Ushuaia.

---

I know the roads in Argentina are going to be challenging so I give myself a break from the scenic roads and hop on a 1,000 mile stretch of highway spanning the Atacama desert in northern Chile. The roads are straight and boring which is a nice change of pace. The frequent roadside memorials is a macabre presence that I can't shake. Some are as simple as a two foot tall white cross and others are open air buildings with large murals of the deceased painted on the walls. The miles are wearing on me and I find myself creeping over the speed limit more and more. The memorials give me a moments pause and I keep my speed in check so I don't end up like so many others.

Giant sand dunes appear out of nowhere and I feel like I've been transported to the Sahara. When I've seen all there is to see in the desert, an amazing landscape strikes awe in me and I spend the day staring off in the distance, soaking in the beauty of the world around me.

There's something off to the right that looks out of place. There is nothing around it and it's far enough away from the road not to be a maintenance building. As I draw closer it looks like a hand. I chalk it up to a desert mirage until I notice a dirt path winding its way towards it. My curiosity gets the most of me and I go off-road to check it out. It turns out to be a giant stone statue that is in fact a hand. It bursts out of the sand like a giant had been buried. Its pinky is the size of a tree trunk and it stands as a monument to something I don't bother to translate. I sit dumbstruck by this sight because I have seen it before. In magazines, documentaries, and on the internet I have seen fellow travelers parked next to this hand. I would sit at home envious of their courage and wherewithal to conquer these exotic places, and now here I am. I feel like I am one of them now, a part of the elite adventure travelers' club.

There is a problem with this though. To paraphrase Woody Allen, "There must be something wrong with any club that would have me for a member". I'm just a stupid schmuck bumbling his way across the continents, and the idea that I am part of the best of the best sounds like hubris. But here I am, in the place where all the other experts have been. I've made it here on my own steam and I'm going all the way to Ushuaia like the rest did. In my mind, I built up other world travelers as a kind of Indiana Jones character, with talents, tricks, or powers that allow them to conquer exotic and foreign lands, but I realize that's bullshit. The world is a kind and accepting place and the journey is a joy, not a cosmic battle. I conquered myself, not the world. My inhibitions, fears, presuppositions, and paranoia have been tested and when I have let them go I've been rewarded with experiences that enrich my character and change my perspective for the better. I ruminate over these ideas for the next few hours before pulling off to camp in the desert.

I am drawing close to Santiago, the capital, and decide to head east toward Argentina to avoid the chaos of the city. I'm off the highways and crawling through back roads. I don't bother looking for a designated campground for the night. I find a section of road with a sharp switchback. No one could keep their eye on the side of the road to notice me sleeping. For good measure, I hide Jenny in some bushes and repel down a slope to hang my hammock for the night.

# DAY 191
# THE ARGENTINIAN BORDER

"It is good to have an end to journey toward;
but it is the journey that matters, in the end."

Ernest Hemingway

Latitude:   032° 49' 35" S
Longitude: 070° 03' 58" W

2,653 miles to Ushuaia

---

The Argentina/Chile border ends up being the fastest crossing I've ever done. It's the last border I will cross before I return home to the US and I savor the sound of the last visa stamp I will hear for a long time. This is it. It is really happening. No more detours. I just have to ride south until I hit the shores of Ushuaia.

There's no alternate routes to consider. I want to ride down Ruta 40, the road everyone talks about. Seventy mile per hour winds are not uncommon through some stretches. As a motorcyclist I know exactly how those kinds of winds feel, and I've adapted to them. I've been the one moving though, and I fantasize about experiencing this phenomenon at a standstill. You start to get moved around in 90 MPH winds, and at 120 you better hang onto something. The highest recorded wind speed is 170 and part of me hopes for a new record. Just give me a ditch to take cover in. It's the debris that kills you, and there's a big shortage of that in the deserts of Patagonia.

I am running out of money and time. I want to return home for an event I participate in every year. It's an expo for adventurous types that like to travel overland with all sorts of vehicles. This event instilled the confidence in me to make this journey in the first place. It's the best kind of homecoming I can imagine so I don't want to miss it.

I pull long days in the saddle to make the most of the daylight and cover as many miles as I can bear. I keep thinking about the sign for Ushuaia and how I will react when I see it. I wonder what is in store for me after all this. I've been a guy on a bike for eight months and the idea of being anything else seems scary. Can I step back into a cubicle? Will the sight of a mini-mall make me run for the hills? Will I lose everything I've become on this wild journey? I've been moving for so long, I wonder how long I can stand still when I get back. Things will work themselves out, I tell myself.

I switch my GPS into its compass mode and watch the needle point south. I haven't calculated the number of miles to Ushuaia. It doesn't matter really and the number will only drive me crazy as I calculate my progress every hour in my head while I read the latest count on my odometer. I compromise instead and use degrees of latitude as my unit of measurement for distance. Ushuaia is at 55 degrees south and I have 20 to go.

At the end of a hard day I sit and look at my maps on my GPS. I'm not planning any routes, I just like looking at them. I reminisce over the places I've been. A squiggly line along a familiar ridge brings me back to that truck blocking the road in Guatemala, a Nicaraguan city reminds me of getting arrested, and the port city in Panama is my entrance to a new continent. The breadcrumbs that log my path are a history book of this vagabond life. It's the best way to tell the story of a life on the move. The book will be closed once I stop moving and the path reaches its end point. My eyes trace the remaining path ahead to Ushuaia, the end of the road and death of this adventure. I have mixed emotions about my arrival.

Then there's that familiar dot that's been blinking at me for almost eight months, my current location. My constantly changing backgrounds of unfamiliar places leaves me wanting for something static. I can always count on my GPS location being there (plus or minus 15 feet), and it brings me some level of comfort. I don't know where the hell I am but at least something does.

The road ahead is completely unknown. It's less terrifying after being on the road for a while. I had to tell myself, "everything is going to be ok" over and over. If you hear something enough times you'll start to believe it no matter how ridiculous. The difference now is that I no longer need convincing. I truly believe that everything is going to be ok. I look over the road ahead on the map and it exhilarates me. I fantasize over who and what might be there. My GPS is like a TV blaring in the background. I turn it off so it doesn't keep me up.

The road is growing more and more difficult. The pavement turns to dirt and conditions become unpredictable. I learned my lesson in Bolivia and I take my time. I am getting impatient and I push myself to stay in the saddle until the sun goes down. I stock up on rice and camp behind hills off the side of the road. I'm not happy, but I'm making my way south and I forfeit my comfort to make the miles. I typically don't take half measures when I set out to do something, and the way I'm behaving is a good example of it. I have two weeks before I need to be on a flight back home and I'm going to make it to Ushuaia.

In the morning I rewrap my knee and ankle. They are still weak from Bolivia, but the swelling in my broken thumb has gone down and I can grasp things without my motorcycle glove on. I ride until dusk and pull off the side of the road. I don't have any energy to set up a proper camp so I take a tarp and fashion a makeshift shelter by attaching one side to the top of Jenny and staking the other side to the ground. I crawl into my bivy sack and snuggle up against her crankcase.

The next day is just like the previous and I have lost all sense of time. I purposely ignore my clock and I have no idea what day it is. I camp in a ditch that night and curl my head inside my bivy sack to escape the unceasing winds.

My morale is in the toilet, but I keep pressing on. When I rest or eat I am filled with anxiety about my lack of movement. My job is to keep Jenny's wheels spinning southbound, and every moment spent doing otherwise feels like a waste of time. I'm on a mission and I neglect my mind and body to complete it.

"If Jenny can keep running, then so can I," I tell myself.

I've placed myself in some perverse contest between man and machine. The road turns back to pavement for 60 miles and it boosts my spirits. I pass through a forest, and around a corner I spot a lake. Its brilliant blue waters leave me spellbound and I stop to stare at its beauty. I've got four more hours of riding I can do before sunset, but I call it quits and find a spot near the lake to camp for the night. The past four days have been filled with eating, sleeping and riding, not much walking. The act of walking around the shore feels foreign to me and I enjoy it while I can before tomorrow.

I have a shirt, slick with oil from a faulty oil cap on a bottle. I've been meaning to clean it for weeks and choose this lake to do it. I plunge it into the clear water and watch the oily rainbow swirls spiral outward. I smile out of reflex at the bright colors, then realize what a schmuck I am. I feel like I've defiled this place, so pure and untouched by humans. I'm ashamed for my ignorance and spend the rest of the evening kicking myself, wondering how my actions affected the environment.

---

With plenty of sleep the previous night I decide to ride to the point of exhaustion. It's late and I'm riding south on Argentina's Ruta 40. My pupils shrink from Jenny's bright headlight hitting the dirt road. The soft full moon illuminates the road better than her artificial light and I want to pull the fuse. I would risk an impact from oncoming traffic so I leave it and continue riding half blind. I am 45 degrees south of the Equator and 10 degrees from my destination. That's about a thousand miles, but I don't use miles as the metric of my progress anymore. Some days of riding yields a degree or two and other days a fraction based on the difficulty of the terrain. It has been 19,000 miles of riding that has brought me so close to the edge of the world, the southernmost point of the Americas. Jenny is falling apart from all I've put her through and her pain is an extension of my own.

I try to keep the throttle steady with my broken thumb. The road is made of a powdery dirt and rocks the size of a fist. This is all by design. It is maintained by dumping more dirt and rock on it. Large trucks pack the loose mixture into a solid footing, but it must have been only a few days since they threw down the last batch. Trucks leave packed dirt tracks, but everything else is a dry mush that Jenny sinks into.

I muddle my way through the night at a slow pace, 30 or 40 MPH at most. There is very little traffic at this time of night, but the few trucks that do pass me kick up a swarm of rocky shrapnel. Complete concentration is required to avoid slipping into the mush. I can stop at any moment and sleep, but I won't. I am so close. The destination I set out for 193 days ago is a few days away. I keep going, draining the last drops of fuel in Jenny and me. My dream is unfolding mile by mile and soon I'll pass the gates into Ushuaia, the city that sits on the bottom of the world.

My eyes flash to the odometer too often.

"Ten more miles."
"OK twenty."

This is the conversation I've had with myself for the past hundred miles until I put a piece of duct tape over the dial. Despite all the trips to welders, Jenny's left luggage rack broke off in Bolivia after all the crashes. She's lopsided with a bag on her tail and the other on her right. Her balance is off and I have to constantly correct it. I've been making an endless left turn for the past three weeks to keep her straight.

Jenny violently veers to the left and before I can do anything to stop it, I realize my right case has rattled free. The corrective steering I've been applying is no longer…correct. At speed we take a dive and slide through the mush. We come to a stop and I'm screaming.

"TRIP OVER! TRIP OVER! TRIP OVER!"

My breath leaves me and I whimper, "I wanna go home."

My leg is pinned and I can't reach the ignition to turn off the lights. After 14 hours of Jenny's single cylinder put-putting in my ear the silence is suffocating me like a vacuum and I lay there trapped, hypnotized by the spin of the rear wheel in the red glow of Jenny's tail light.

After a couple of minutes of grunting and yelling I free my leg. I perform the post-crash tasks I'm too familiar with: lift Jenny up, check for signs of damage, then disrobe and check for signs of injuries. She's been my best friend throughout this crazy journey. I stumble back down the road along a small trail of impact craters created by the toppling of my luggage end over end. The case is resting right side up as if it had been placed there deliberately.

I calm down and replay the guttural scream after the crash over and over in my head. Should I stop now? Can I? I watch an imaginary game of tennis. Right, then left, over and over. One side, the destination I had dreamed of reaching for three years, and the other is home. I am a couple of bus rides and a plane ticket away from escaping this self-made hell. Should I turn my back on the place I've been traveling to for over seven months? I am only a thousand miles away, a week tops.

I push Jenny into a ditch and call it a day. Hours pass and I'm still sitting on the side of the road, not sleeping like I should be, considering my options.

I am battered physically, emotionally, and mechanically. I'm chasing an arbitrary goal and pushing myself way too hard to reach it.

I have to consider whether I can safely make it. Am I pushing Jenny and myself beyond our boundaries?

"What's in Ushuaia?" countless people have asked me.
"I don't know, but I'm more concerned with what's in between here and there," I always say.

I question whether I can make it there safely. I have to keep pushing myself like this if I am going to make it back on time. The whole situation reeks of desperation and risk. And for what? To say that I made it to the bottom of South America. The past five days have been hell, and I have seven more ahead. The gas station attendant 12 miles back keeps popping in my head. We were talking about bikes and he really liked mine. I wonder if he would buy Jenny.

"It's the journey, not the destination," they say.
"What am I doing?"
"Is this worth it?"

A few hours pass and I watch the full moon circle overhead.

"I want to go home," I say aloud.

I just have to say it once, and I know my decision is right.

The trip is over. I'm going home.

# DAY 195
# PATAGONIA, ARGENTINA

"A good traveler has no fixed plans and is not intent on arriving."

Lao Tzu

Latitude:   045° 07' 59" S
Longitude: 070° 41' 39" W

1,057 miles to Ushuaia

---

I wake with my head nestled between Jenny's front tire and her engine. Last night felt like a dream, and I wake up refreshed. Now that both of my luggage racks are broken I stack my cases precariously high on Jenny's tail. It's only twelve slow miles back to that gas station where I can try and sell Jenny for a plane ticket home. I start riding and notice the morning sun shining on my right shoulder. It had been on my left shoulder throughout this whole journey and reality of heading north hits me.

I remind myself of all the things I came to a realization about under last night's moon. I'm rushing to get to a destination that doesn't matter. The journey is what matters. It sucks and is getting hazardous. It's not enjoyable, and it's not always supposed to be, but it has spiraled to the point where I want it to end. Ushuaia has always been an arbitrary destination I chose and I'm killing myself over it. Continuing for the sake of a journey feels perverse to me in these circumstances. It took the crash for me to pause and realize I'm pushing myself beyond my limits for nothing. I've already had an amazing journey that has been personally transformative. I'm 1,000 miles away from the destination I've pointed Jenny's front wheel towards for seven months, and I have no regrets turning my back on it.

I arrive at the gas station and Lucas, the owner, is surprised to see me back so soon. He only has to see my face and the natural question follows.

"What's wrong?" he asks.

"I had a crash, and I'm done traveling. I would like to sell my bike and hop a train to Buenos Aires,." I say.

"Are you ok?"

"Yes, I'm fine. I'm just very tired after all these months, and I don't want to continue."

"Come inside."

He prepares lunch for Franco, his son, and me as we chat about everything but Jenny for an hour. Franco is eight, and shy, but he comes around and is full of energy after ten minutes. Lucas opens a beer for me without asking. He knows I need one.

Lucas is very interested in Jenny, but can't get over the lack of paperwork that would facilitate a proper sale of an imported motorcycle. He calls some friends and a few hours later a man arrives, kicking Jenny's tires and taking her for a spin. We reach an agreement and I hand over the keys.

"Wait, one minute!" I say.

I take a moment to remove the blanket secured to Jenny's saddle that I bought in Guatemala. I try not to get attached to things, but I can't resist holding onto this keepsake. I check into a hotel and my first call is to Amber.

"Honey?" I ask.

"What's wrong?" she immediately asks. She knows from my personal locator beacon that I haven't moved for the past two days.

"It's over. I'm on my way home."

"What happened?"

"I had another crash, and I'm ok, I didn't get hurt, but it made me realize I can't keep doing this anymore."

"You're so close though!"

"I know, but it doesn't matter. I'm done, and I'm totally okay with it. I'm coming home sweetie."

I only have to say it once and she doesn't try and convince me otherwise.

---

I wake up at five o'clock to catch a bus taking me to Comodoro on the east coast. From there a 23 hour bus ride will take me to Buenos Aires where I will board a plane taking me back to Phoenix where I started this whole journey. I rummage through my luggage and determine what I can feasibly carry. I start piling discarded items in a corner, and pack my valuables in two luggage cases and a duffle bag.

I pack away all my motorcycle gear except for my gloves. As I walk from the hotel to the bus station under the weight of my duffle on my back, I grasp the luggage cases and take small, calculated steps as the handles dig into the palms of my gloved hands.

I sit at the empty station an hour early, and the finality of my journey is setting in. I am filled with doubt and wonder if I made the right decision. The decision has been made so there's no use worrying about it. I board the bus and the beginning of the end starts.

At Comodoro I switch to a bus bound for Buenos Aires. I watch the dot on my GPS creep north, the first time I am moving away from Ushuaia. Doubt and insecurity amplifies with each mile. Maybe I could have made it. I feel better now. Maybe I just needed a few days rest. Maybe my decision was made in haste. After sitting for hours I stand to stretch my legs, and I'm reminded of my twisted ankle, sprained knee and broken thumb. The shooting pain dissipates my doubt.

Browsing the maps in my GPS, I'm reminded of all the amazing things I've seen and people I've met. The generous hosts, the shakedown in Mexico, the jungles of Guatemala, the national news coverage, getting arrested in Nicaragua, the sea voyage to Colombia, the thrill of the Andes and the challenge of Bolivia. What I've experienced is so much more than I could have imagined. A motorcycle passes our bus on the highway and I wish I were back with Jenny. She's gone and I have a new adventure ahead of me: assimilating back into Western society.

I have three days in Buenos Aires before my flight so I check into a comfortable hotel and enjoy the hot water. I pack up in preparation for a departure that won't come for a few days. The habits of a vagabond on the move are tough to kick.

I walk the streets and they feel different. I wear my motorcycle boots for their familiarity. I'm a biker without a bike, and it's hard to wrap my head around this. I pass a movie theater and see the next available showing of anything. The visuals and sound consume my senses as if this were my first time in the theater.

There are a million things to be done in the city but I'm done seeing what's to be seen and doing what must be done.

My plane departs in the afternoon and I take a walk through a park in the morning. I sit and watch men playing chess and soon I'm invited to play. The first game is fast and ends with a blunder I make in the heat of the moment. The second game is slow and I gain an upper hand mid game. There's no chess clock to time the game but I glance at my watch frequently, anxious over my time running out before I must go. My preoccupation costs me my queen. I tip my king over and the game is over. Assessing futile situations and knowing when to call it quits is a valuable skill I've developed.

I watch the Earth roll beneath the wings of the aircraft and I ponder over the nature of travel regarding its mode. The more efficient a mode of travel is, the less connected you are with the land you are traversing. The slower you travel the richer your experiences will be. The more Jenny or the road slowed me down, the more fun I had. It's only until I am airborne that I realize this.

Fourteen hours later I am standing on the curb at Sky Harbor airport in Phoenix and the familiarity of this once distance place warps my reality. Was my former life a dream, or the journey? Am I waking up or falling asleep? The first familiar face in three months pulls up to the curb and I hop in the car.

"I need to call Homeland Security, the DEA or something. Can I use your phone?"

"What?" my friend asks.

"Remember that whole thing with the Mexican cops?"

"Yea."

"Well I have some reason to believe they may be connected to a drug cartel, and I may have inadvertently pissed them off. Maybe I should tell my situation to someone in case..."

I can't say it.

"In case what?" my friend asks.

"In case I am in any danger."

"Oh. Yea, here," he says, and hands me his phone.

I dial the numbers I jotted down four months ago to call when I arrive back in the US. The boogeymen that formed in my mind back in Guatemala, when my video went viral, have resurfaced.

"I'm sure it's nothing. I would probably be dead already if they wanted it that way."

I laugh but my friend doesn't join me.

I am bounced from a switchboard operator at Homeland Security to the CIA, then to the DEA and back to Homeland Security. I quickly give up.

"I'm probably overreacting."

I open my notebook to a page where I have a list of tasks once home. It reads:

Activate cell phone
Start repaying student loans
Oil change

It takes me a while, but I drag my pen across the page slowly and deliberately along the last item:

Assess threat to life.

# EPILOGUE

North of Phoenix is an annual gathering of travel enthusiasts involving any vehicle you can imagine. I attended this event three years ago and it boosted my confidence before venturing out into the world alone. I wasn't the only weirdo wanting to head out into the unknown. These people were my evidence against the naysayers who thought I would be shot on sight, and I can't wait to reunite with them and share my stories. I planned my return to coincide with this event.

I bump into Lorraine Chittock, a vibrant woman whose smile lights up a room. She's been traveling around the world for more than two decades.

"Hi Lorraine," I say quietly when I notice her in a crowd. "Bill!" she says, and throws her arms around me, "how are you?!"

"I am really good."

She steps back and her face investigates mine.

"You've changed," she says with a straight face.

"What?" I ask.

"You've changed. I can see it."

The lifetime of our relationship is about two hours long, just a few conversations here and there. Despite this she sees what most don't.

"Well yea, I've grown a beard," I say.

"No, not that. You just got back didn't you?"

"I did."

"I want to hear everything, but your smile already speaks volumes."

"Thanks Lorraine."

These kind of moments happen throughout the three-day

weekend and I feel home again.

---

Amber moved to Philadelphia and I am following her there. I'm excited to see her but I want to rest as well. I still have a limp from Bolivia and the last thing I want to do is ride 2,400 miles on Marla, my sport bike, but two days after the gathering of travelers ends I am on a cross-country trek from the southwest to the northeast. Four horrible days later I am circling blocks on the streets of Philly, looking for Amber's apartment. A door opens and her bright smile follows. She recognizes the sound of Marla and I grin ear to ear inside my helmet when I see her face. I've been sleeping at rest stops and haven't changed my clothes since Phoenix. I come inside and she orders me to take my clothes off, but not in the good way. As if they were radioactive, she collects my stinky garments in a garbage bag and double bags it. I manage to offend Amber with my odor, despite her being exposed to Philadelphia, dubbed the dirtiest city in America.

The habits of a traveler are tough to kick. I wake up in the morning, and need a moment to remember where I am. It's the same place as yesterday…weird. I pack a liter of water, my GPS, personal locator beacon, 100 feet of rope, and my knife. There's no telling what will happen on the way to the coffee shop. Amber comes home to underwear and socks soaking in the bathroom sink. I forget I have more than three pairs and we have a washer. I am shocked by the accessibility of simple items.

"Honey! This place has toothpaste, blenders and skis all under one roof!"

She smiles and nods. I'm more cheap than I used to be, which I didn't think was possible. I cringe when I pay four dollars for coffee and compare it to the cost of a hotel in Guatemala. I spend a month recovering from my injuries and enjoy staying in one place. Another month passes and I am back in a boring office, but luckily it's only part time and still pays the bills. My anxiety medication has run out so I'm sitting in a waiting room with the rest of south Philly who can't afford mental health care. I go through an initial interview with a woman to assess what kind of care I need. She wants to know about my history and runs through your run-of-the-mill horrors.

"Any instances of substance abuse? What about sexual abuse? Have you been exposed to graphic violence? Have you been a victim of violence? How was your family life growing up?"

"Nope. Nah. No. Nope. My family life was good," I answer.

"Have you ever been in a life threatening situation?" she asks.

"Nope. Well, actually..."

The room gets very quiet.

"Technically, yes," I answer.

"Technically?" she asks.

"I fell off my motorcycle at 80mph. It sounds worse than it is."

The pace of her pen picks up, telling me she's no longer just making "X"s in a checkbox.

"Also there was this police bribe situation in Mexico, and I got them fired. Some say they may have been connected with a cartel, but I don't know. So there's that. It's probably nothing at this point and if it was a real threat I'd probably be dead already."

"Anything else?" she asks while looking up from her pad of paper.

"Then there's Bolivia where I had a fairly low-speed crash at 40mph, but it was the scariest and most painful mishap along the way."

She continues taking notes and we finish the rest of the initial evaluation.

"What's next?" I ask.

"Your information will be forwarded to our staff who will choose a specific psychiatrist for you to see, but I'm pretty sure I know the guy you're going to get," she says with a smile.

Next week I arrive early to my appointment with the doctor, to get this song and dance over with so I can get my medication and get on with life. I'm given vague directions to the doctor's office and I walk steadily down a hallway, sheepishly pausing at each doorway to see if I am expected.

"Come in Mr. Dwyer!" I hear from behind a desk.

He has a commanding voice, and silver hair. He shuffles through my file and I sit down looking around the room.

"What brings you here?"
"I have a history of anxiety and depression. I am running out of medication so I'm here to get more."
"Let's back up before we talk medication."

I've been to enough mental health professionals so my background story sounds rehearsed. It can take four minutes or five sessions to get all the crucial information conveyed, but I took notes of my condition over the years and recite the episodic bullet points with little effort. I save my motorcycle journey for last, the thing I know he'll be the most interested in, the thing that will distract from a discussion about my mental health.

His office walls are covered with motorcycle memorabilia and a blown up photo of his son sitting on a dirt bike from his motocross days. He asks what I've been doing lately and I spill the news about my journey through Latin America. He brings up a recent trip he took to Alaska and for the next half hour we are swapping stories.

The session is going way over our allotted time and phone calls from reception are met with a grimace and a careless attitude that only an old man can get away with. The receptionist knocks on the door and we're forced to wrap things up.

"Can I get a prescription?" I ask as I stand up to leave.

"Sure, what do you want?"

I feel I need to justify what I ask for, so I drill through my medication history and he's getting visibly antsy.

"What was the last medication you were on?"

"Celexa. Do you think I should continue with that?"

"If it worked for you, sure. How many do you want?"

"As much as you can so I can save money by refilling less. Is that ok?" I ask sheepishly.

"Sure. You're going to do what you want with these anyways."

---

As I cross the street a car speeds up to make the light, cutting close in front of me. I see it all happening and don't slow down. My arm cartwheels back and my fist lands on the back of the car. The car stops up ahead and the driver gets out.

"What?!" I shout.

They drive away. The driver made a dick move, but I didn't have to do what I did. What was the point? Adjusting back to an American lifestyle is difficult for me, and my doctor sees this before I do.

"Do you have any goals or aspirations?" he asks.

"God no," I say with recoil.

"Why not?" he asks.

"I used to be all about goals. I'm sick of having a set of never ending goals."

"Goals can be important sometimes."

"My only goal is to figure out how to get back out on the road and have no direction. That's where I belong."

"You and me both."

He goes on to talk about another trip and we spend the next half hour talking shop until the receptionist is barging through the door to remind us that our time is up.

I spend a lot of time walking around the city in my motorcycle boots. Their weight slows down the frantic pace I usually have. I stop to look at my surroundings often and I write in my journal. Springtime comes and my feet sweat too much to bear the heat, so I swap them for a pair of sneakers. I expect my pace to quicken without the burdensome weight of a motorcycle boot. My feet are free to flail at their normal hurried pace, but I stroll with a relaxed gait, and wonder why.

I begin caring less about the things that normally worry me. I don't like shoes and walk around in socks at the office. A co-worker pulls me aside and let's me know the director would freak out if she saw me like this. I decide not to let fear alter my natural behavior and continue doing so until this "what if" becomes a reality.

Social situations feel natural for me now. I don't give canned answers to questions like "How are you?" and react genuinely rather than with a reactive response of "Good!" I don't have to prep myself before an evening out with new friends, preoccupying myself with how we can connect and what topics can I discuss to avoid awkward silence. When there is silence it doesn't feel awkward anymore anyways.

I'm coming to terms with not being a traveler anymore. I start writing about moments on the road before they fade away. I toy with the prospect of writing a book, but ignore the idea of a finished work and keep writing with no purpose in mind. I'm more concerned with what happened to me. Lorraine was right, I have changed, but I can't identify its nature.

I pour over the stories from the road and it feels like fiction at times. Who was this guy? Was this me? The Mexican bribe, the Guatemalan back roads, the Nicaraguan arrest, the open ocean, the Andes, the Bolivian highlands and Patagonia. I never thought I had the capacity to overcome these challenges, or react in the ways I had.

I feel like I've performed a rite of passage and see the world with new eyes.

I endured a series of psychological battles involving my relationship with the world. It's no longer a thing to overcome or fear. I traveled through the world on two wheels, vulnerable to its elements, terrain and people. I've heard something spoken with sincerity from those who have seen the world so intimately. Hearing this gave me confidence to go out into the world myself, and now I can repeat this to others and mean it:

The world is a safe place.

I walk the streets of Philadelphia with the eyes of a foreigner in the same boots that carried me to Argentina. I don't know how I will adjust to my old lifestyle. I'm not obsessively preoccupied with future uncertainties like I once was. I'm not endlessly analyzing what course of action to take that will yield the most optimal result. My anxiety has subsided to a level I've never experienced before. There is no one moment on my journey I can attribute to this improvement, but it is undoubtedly the source. All the therapy and medication in the world couldn't have had the same effect that this journey had on me. I walk to nowhere with an ease in my step and peace in my mind. I have no expectations or prospects for my life and what comes next. Whatever happens, I know the world will provide me with a path and I will be strong enough to take it. Most importantly, I remind myself:

Everything will be ok.

But there is one thing that worries me. I've been on the move for so long, the idea of standing still puts me on edge. I have a new city to discover, and all that is new will eventually turn familiar because this city is my new home. On the road, I've lived with an intensity like never before, and like an addict, I want to sustain the high of the road here at home.

I fear I'll turn back into the miserable person I once was, as if traveling was the only thing keeping all this at bay. The constant challenge of being exposed to the unfamiliar has made me a stronger person, but the idea of a routine and things having familiarity scares the hell out of me. I spent so much time and energy changing my surroundings that I hadn't noticed the positive change in myself. After a while I find the virtue in the familiar and the urge to run off to a new land isn't in the forefront of my mind. For the first time in my life, I rest easy and feel comfortable on two feet rather than two wheels.

# FOLLOW MY NEXT ADVENTURE

atlasrider.com

Website:        atlasrider.com
Facebook:       facebook.com/AtlasRiderCom
Twitter:        twitter.com/AtlasRider
YouTube:        youtube.com/AtlasRider

# LIFETIME ACCESS TO
# FUTURE EDITIONS

I plan on releasing new editions of *Anxiety Across the Americas* that include multimedia components like photo and video. I don't want to penalize readers who happened to buy an early edition by forcing them to buy later editions containing additional value to the story, so I will be providing access to the new editions to people like you who have purchased the older editions. To be notified of the availability of future editions you can sign up for alerts at the following website:

http://www.atlasrider.com/new-edition/

Thanks for supporting independent authors like myself.